Abraham
Lincoln

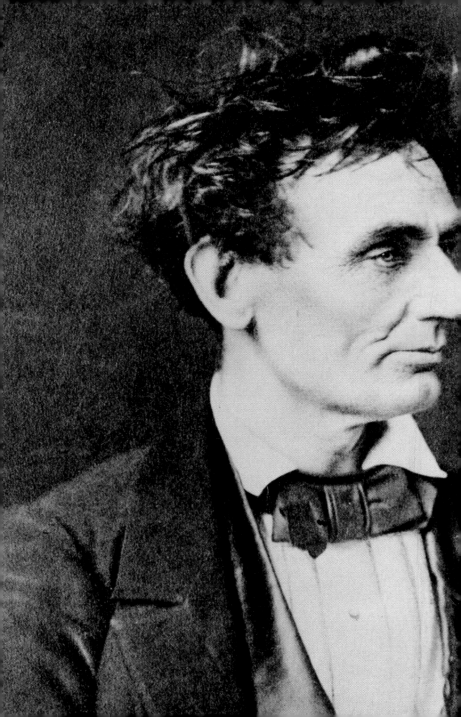

Abraham Lincoln

Tanya Lee Stone

DK PUBLISHING, INC.

LONDON, NEW YORK, MUNICH,
MELBOURNE, AND DELHI

Designed for DK Publishing
by Mark Johnson Davies

Publishing Director : Beth Sutinis

Art Director : Dirk Kaufman

Creative Director : Tina Vaughan

Photo Research : Anne Burns Images

Production : Chris Avgherinos, Ivor Parker

DTP Designer : Milos Orlovic

First American Edition, 2005

05 06 07 08 09 10 9 8 7 6 5 4 3 2 1
Published in the United States
by DK Publishing, Inc.
375 Hudson St., New York, New York 10014

DK books are available at special discounts for bulk purchases
for sales promotions, premiums, fund-raising, or educational use.
For details, contact:
DK Publishing Special Markets
375 Hudson Street
New York, NY 10014
SpecialSales@dk.com

Published in Great Britain by
Dorling Kindersley Limited.

Library of Congress Cataloging-in-Publication Data
Stone, Tanya Lee.
DK biography: Abraham Lincoln / written by Tanya Lee Stone.-- 1st
American ed.
p. cm. -- (DK biography)
Includes bibliographical references and index.
ISBN 0-7566-0834-1 (pb) -- ISBN 0-7566-0833-3 (plc)
1. Lincoln, Abraham, 1809-1865--Juvenile literature. 2. Presidents--
United States--Biography--Juvenile literature. I. Title: Abraham
Lincoln. II. Title. III. Series.
E457.905.S76 2004
973.7'092--dc22
                              2004024075

Color reproduction by GRB Editrice, Italy
Printed and bound in the United States of America by
WORZALLA, Stevens Point, Wisconsin

Photography credits:
Front cover: Bettmann/CORBIS; Back cover: Alan Schein
Photography/CORBIS; Half-title page: Bettman;
Title page: Historic Photo Collection, Harpers Ferry NHP

Discover more at
www.dk.com

Contents

A Note to My Readers:

History is a tricky thing. The circumstances of any event a person retells are seen through his or her own unique set of eyes. The truth is; it is practically unavoidable for history not to be colored by the people who write about it. And Lincoln is one of the most written about figures in American history. But I promise you this: I have done careful research. I have studied scholarly works about Lincoln and the Civil War. I have considered the sources of the words I have read. And I have worked hard to present a balanced view of the events that affected Lincoln's life.

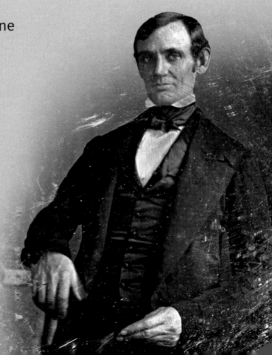

A Nation's Fascination

Twelve funerals. A funeral procession journeying for days through as many cities. Crowds viewing the president's lifeless body in a temporary vault in an Illinois cemetery. The body being moved to a temporary tomb. Then a second tomb. People peeking into the coffin to verify that Lincoln was really inside it. Kidnappers trying to steal the body and hold it for ransom. And finally, laying the sixteenth president to rest where he could no longer be disturbed: under many feet of concrete in the Lincoln Tomb.

The Lincoln Tomb in Springfield, Illinois, is where Abraham Lincoln still rests today, along with his wife Mary and three of their sons—Thomas (called Tad); William (Willie); and Edward (Eddie). A tall obelisk, bronze statues, plaques, and flags also make up this memorial to Abraham Lincoln.

Another major memorial—the Lincoln Memorial—is in Washington, D.C. It was dedicated on February 12, 1922. More than 50,000 people attended. Among them, as an honored guest, was Lincoln's only living son, Robert. The Lincoln Memorial is an impressive place, designed to resemble a Greek temple. Thirty-six columns represent the number of

states in the Union when Lincoln died. In the center chamber sits an enormous marble statue of a seated Lincoln.

So why does a man who died more than 140 years ago still capture our attention—and our hearts? Maybe it is because he was a man who was not afraid to make mistakes, a man who would never pretend to know something when he didn't, a man who worked tirelessly to figure out solutions to difficult problems, and a man who continued to learn and grow throughout his life. Or maybe it is because, truly and deeply, with all his heart, Abraham Lincoln believed in the ideals that the Founding Fathers put forth. He believed in the strength of the Union. He believed in an America in which all people are given the chance to better themselves and make a good life. He believed in the Declaration of Independence that stated, "all Men are created equal, that they are endowed by their Creator with certain unalienable Rights, that among these are Life, Liberty and the Pursuit of Happiness." And he believed in a nation in which even a poor boy from the wilds of Kentucky could grow up to become president of the United States.

1

A Complex Boy

On a cold winter morning, deep in the woods of Kentucky, the sun rose over snow-covered ground. Inside the tiny log cabin, a few streams of light likely peeked through the one window, spilling onto the hard dirt floor. On the cabin's bearskin-covered bed, the dawn ushered a new baby into the world. It was February 12, 1809. The baby was named Abraham Lincoln, after his grandfather, who had been killed by Indians in 1786. In this place near Nolin Creek, his first childhood home, little Abraham learned to walk.

Within two years, Abraham's father, Thomas, in search of better farmland, moved his family a few miles away, to Knob Creek. As he grew, young Abraham climbed trees and fished in the creek. He helped his father with the farmwork, too.

Lincoln's grandfather was killed by Indians. The child lying beside him is Lincoln's father.

One Saturday afternoon, Abraham trudged after Thomas, up and down, up and down the hilly cornfield rows. While Thomas hoed the land, Abraham did as he was told, dropping pumpkin seeds in between the corn. It was tiring work for a little boy. On Sunday, heavy rains fell and washed all that work away. When Abraham Lincoln later recalled his childhood, this was his earliest memory.

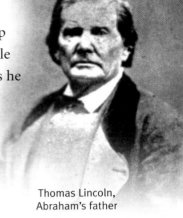

Thomas Lincoln, Abraham's father

Abraham's father was a hardworking farmer and skilled carpenter. He was a popular, lively man who had a lot of friends, and he loved to entertain them with funny stories. Like most Americans who lived during this time, Thomas's family had once owned slaves from Africa. But over time, the issue of slavery began to bother him more and more. He and Abraham's mother, Nancy Hanks Lincoln, even left their church to join a new one led by ministers who were antislavery.

During the time the Lincolns lived in Knob Creek, Nancy gave birth to another son. His name was Thomas, but he lived for only a few days. Thomas was buried near the family's cabin.

Unlike Abraham's father, Nancy Lincoln was a sad, quiet woman. The death of little Thomas likely worsened her condition. Although she could not read, Nancy thought it was important for her children to get some kind of education.

The cabin at Knob Creek, Kentucky, Lincoln's birthplace.

She would sit with Abraham and his older sister, Sarah, reciting passages from the Bible she had memorized. And when Abraham and Sarah were able to take a break from their work on the farm, Nancy encouraged them to walk the two miles, through streams and woods, to the closest schoolhouse. There, Abraham began to learn his letters.

When Abraham was seven, his father moved the family to the free state of Indiana, where slavery wasn't allowed and land was cheap. In 1816, this part of the country was wild and untamed. There were no roads to drive on and no stores to buy supplies from along the way. Imagine putting everything your entire family owns onto the

Slavery in America

At the time of Lincoln's birth, slavery had existed in America for nearly 200 years. It was most popular in the South, where landowners had large farms called plantations. It was cheaper to buy slaves than to hire workers to tend these farms. During the Revolutionary War (1775–1783), people started to feel it was wrong to own slaves in a nation fighting for personal freedom. In the early 1800s, people began to fight against slavery. They were called abolitionists.

backs of two horses. Then imagine constantly having to stop to chop your way through the trees and brush with an ax, cutting a path through the wilderness. Imagine, still, that once you arrive at the end of this long, exhausting journey, there is no house waiting for you. No cozy bed. No warm kitchen. Instead, all you see are more trees. Your father tells you this piece of land seems good for building. And you must work alongside him. You help chop more trees, clear the land, build the cabin, and do other chores. As before, everything you and your family eat must either be grown or killed.

During the next few winter months, while the cabin is being built, your family sleeps in a three-sided shelter. A fire keeps some of the chill away, as does the

Abraham Lincoln's youth and young manhood was spent in the region that is now known as the Midwest.

bearskin in which you wrap yourself. At night, you can hear the wolves howling and bobcats prowling nearby; there are no walls or locked doors to keep you safe. Most of your time is spent trying to stay warm and fed. Whenever there is a break from the work, you are able to get a little bit of schooling done. But you have to walk miles through the wild woods to reach the schoolhouse.

This is what Abraham's life was like then.

As you have probably imagined, Abraham did not much enjoy this time of his life. Just after his eighth birthday, the new cabin near Pigeon Creek was ready. He slept in a loft reached by climbing pegs his father had built into the wall.

There was constant work to be done on the farm. In the spring there were fields to plow, logs to split into rails, and fences to build with them. Although he was only eight, Abraham was strong and good with an ax, and Thomas often had him help with the heavy work. Imagine how hard it must have been to make absolutely everything your family needs to survive in the middle of what was, just a few months before, nothing but thick forest!

Lincoln's childhood home in Indiana is preserved at the Lincoln Boyhood National Memorial.

Everyone, including the children, had to work most of the time. Shortly after the family moved in, Abraham shot a turkey, which was used for the family's dinner. He hated doing it and said he never wanted to kill anything again.

The following year, though, things started looking up for young Abraham. His mother's relatives Thomas and Elizabeth Sparrow moved nearby, bringing

Lincoln's cousins, Dennis (left) and John Hanks (a cousin of Nancy's who moved in with the Lincolns in 1823 (right)), were photographed beside the old Lincoln home in 1865.

with them Abraham's 18-year-old cousin Dennis Hanks. Although Dennis was much older than Abraham, the two boys got along well. In addition to their chores, they managed to find time to fish, swim in the creek, and run barefoot through the woods.

But come summer a terrible illness swept through the area. This "milk sickness" took the lives of the Sparrows. Dennis moved into the loft with Abraham. Then Abraham's mother also got sick and died. She was only 34 years old. Abraham was not yet 10. It was a miserable time. Sarah was just two years older than Abraham, but with her mother gone, she had to take over caring for the family. She tried her best to

MILK SICKNESS

It was later discovered that milk sickness came from cows that grazed on the white snakeroot plant, which poisoned the milk people drank.

cook and clean, but sometimes she would just sit down by the fire and cry.

The following year, Thomas Lincoln, in need of a new wife and mother for his family, traveled to Kentucky to marry an old friend named Sarah Bush Johnston. She was a widow and had three children of her own. (That meant eight people were about to share the tiny Lincoln home!) Sally, as she was called, arrived at the Lincoln home in Pigeon Creek to find hungry, ragged children and a filthy, gloomy cabin in desperate need of her attention. She was kind and sweet, and Abraham took to her right away. Sally made the difference between night and day—everything in Abraham's childhood seemed better once she came into his life. He even called her "Mama."

Abraham's ax-swinging talents had prompted his father to hire him out to work for other homesteaders. He and Thomas even helped build the Pigeon Creek Baptist Church. The preacher there was known for being antislavery. When Abraham was 14, his parents and sister joined the church. Like his father, Abraham felt slavery was wrong. But he did not want to join the church.

Lincoln's mother, Nancy Hanks, died in 1818. This stone was placed at her grave after 1865.

However, his father arranged for him to work sweeping out the church and stocking it with candles. It is likely that Abraham listened to the sermons, too. He would sometimes stand outside the church, on top of a tree stump, and mock the preacher's words to the laughter of his friends. If his father came upon such a scene, he would make Abraham stop and send him back to his work.

Abraham Lincoln's stepmother, Sarah Bush Johnston. She and Abraham were very close.

Although Abraham was good at the manual labor his father had him doing, he did not like it. He much preferred making everyone around him laugh by telling raucous stories and jokes. And once he learned to read, he preferred that over most things.

Sally and Thomas believed education was important and sent all their children to school whenever they could spare them. As a boy, Abraham was not noted for being particularly smart. But Sally could see that he was; he simply had a different way of learning. He wasn't fast, but he worked at what he wanted to learn with a passion. And once he knew something, he never forgot it. Sally said, "…he must understand everything—even to the smallest thing—minutely and exactly—he would then repeat it over to

15

A page from Abraham's schoolbook shows multiplication and division exercises.

himself again and again…and when it was fixed in his mind to suit him he became easy and he never lost that fact or his understanding of it."

There was not always a school to go to, but from the time he was 11, Abraham attended school anytime there was a chance to break away from chores. There never was much time. By his fifteenth year, the total amount of formal education Abraham had managed to fit in was less than a year. Even so, he became an excellent speller and had learned to read and write. Neighbors who couldn't read or write asked him to write letters for them. He even had a penchant for writing poetry. On a page in his arithmetic book he wrote:

> *Abraham Lincoln*
> *his hand and pen*
> *he will be good but*
> *god knows when*

Each day, Abraham went about his work with a book stashed away, just in case a moment for a reading break should appear. He would sit right down in a field while his horse rested, for example, and open his book. Hearing of this habit, some people thought he was lazy. Even at the end of a long, tiring day, Abraham would sit in a corner and read. He read every book he could get his hands on. Some of his favorites were *Aesop's Fables*, *The Life of Washington*, *The Arabian Nights*, and *Robinson Crusoe*.

By the time Abraham was 16, he was six feet tall. His buckskin pants were always too short and several inches of bare leg stuck out at the bottoms. He may have been self-conscious about his looks, so tall and lean with an angular face. He often seemed sad and shy—especially around girls. But he could be funny and lively, too. And he was known for being a strong wrestler and a fast runner. In what was to be a lifelong personality trait, young Abraham was popular with many, but close to hardly anyone, including his father. The two just didn't seem to understand each other and grew further and further apart.

Young Abraham read whenever he got a chance.

2

Ordinary and Extraordinary

O ther things were distancing Abraham from home, too.
His sister Sarah married a neighbor, Aaron Grigsby,
and moved out. His stepsister Matilda also married and
moved away. At 17, Abraham felt fewer ties to home. He went
to work for a man named James Taylor, helping with his
ferryboat business on the Ohio River. He also plowed and
built fences. Abraham was earning about $6 a month. He used
his spare time to build a flatboat of his own. When it was finished,
two men asked him to take them out to a steamer ship coming
down the river. He later recalled how he felt when they paid
him for his trouble. "...I could scarcely
believe...that I, a poor boy, had earned a
dollar in less than a day....The world

Lincoln working as a
ferryman on the
Mississippi River.

seemed wider and fairer before me. I was a more hopeful and confident being from that time."

But a sad blow was about to hit him hard. On January 20, 1828, his sister Sarah died giving birth to her first child. The following April, Abraham left Pigeon Creek. Although he would return for a short time, he never called it home again. Lincoln was 19 years old. James Gentry hired him to take a flatboat full of produce and supplies all the way to New Orleans. Lincoln made the trip with Allen Gentry, one of Gentry's sons. They traveled 1,200 miles down the Ohio River and the Mississippi. The waters of the Ohio are calm, but the Mighty Mississippi earns every letter of its nickname. Changing currents, tangled banks, and sandbars made for a dangerous journey. When Lincoln and Gentry got to Baton Rouge, Louisiana, the excitement grew. Their boat was attacked by slaves trying to steal their cargo. The two young men managed to save their goods and shove off for New Orleans.

New Orleans was by far the busiest place Lincoln had seen. The port was teeming with hundreds of boats. Cargo was piled up on docks and men were loading and unloading as fast as they could. The shops were bustling. French and English could both be heard. The streets were jammed with people of all kinds. Lincoln saw slave markets for the first time. Groups of men stood on one side and women on the other as families were torn apart and sold like cattle.

In March 1830, Lincoln helped his father move to Illinois.

Slave auctions, such as the one in this detail of a painting by Thomas Satterwhite Noble, were common in the mid-1800s. Lincoln saw one for the first time when he went to New Orleans.

Again he worked with Thomas to build a log cabin, split rails for making fences, clear land, and plant crops. Then a hard, cold winter set in. Lincoln was itching to make a life for himself. He, cousin John Hanks, and stepbrother John Johnston decided to work for Denton Offutt in the spring. Offutt had a flatboat and wanted the men to take a load of goods to New Orleans. But when they met up with Offutt, there was no flatboat. This didn't stop Lincoln. He made up his mind they would build it themselves—and so they did. By April 1831, they were on their way.

The Sangamon River would take them to the Illinois River and then on to the Mississippi. But the Sangamon was so low Lincoln constantly had to avoid getting tangled in branches and stuck on sandbars. In New Salem, Illinois, they did get stuck. Then the boat began to fill with water. That boat was loaded with wheat, corn, and pork. They couldn't afford to lose the cargo!

Lincoln climbed onto the riverbank and tried to shift the weight of the boat—but it would not move. Then he had an idea. They unloaded some cargo onto the bank.

Then Lincoln got a hand drill from New Salem village, made a hole to let out the water, stopped it back up, and tried to shove off again. This time it worked! Offutt, who had come along for the ride, was impressed—both with Lincoln and with the little village of New Salem. Offutt thought it was a good place to open up a general store, as he predicted steamboats would start coming by on a regular basis. He offered Lincoln a job running the store when he returned from New Orleans. In July 1831, Lincoln arrived back in New Salem. He was 22.

But in keeping with Offutt's unreliable nature, there *was* no store yet. In the meantime, Lincoln looked for odd jobs. The hardworking Lincoln had no trouble finding work, and the storytelling Lincoln had no trouble finding friends. He had never lived in a place with so many people before—nearly 100. He took to New Salem quickly—and it took to him. When Offutt's store opened in September, he settled in.

Lincoln, along with John Hanks and John Johnston (in back), talks to Denton Offutt about a job.

The educated people of the town, such as schoolmaster Mentor Graham, were impressed with Lincoln's eagerness to continue his

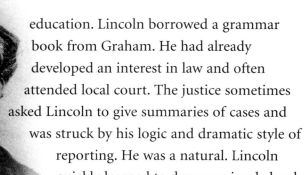

education. Lincoln borrowed a grammar book from Graham. He had already developed an interest in law and often attended local court. The justice sometimes asked Lincoln to give summaries of cases and was struck by his logic and dramatic style of reporting. He was a natural. Lincoln quickly learned to draw up simple legal documents and did so for several townspeople. James Rutledge, who started the New Salem Debating Society, lent books to Lincoln and invited him to debate. Lincoln was good at it, growing in confidence as he debated topics with passion.

Mentor Graham helped Abraham learn to become a surveyor.

Lincoln had brains and brawn, as Offutt liked to brag. He set him up to wrestle the toughest of the Clary's Grove gang that often came to town—Jack Armstrong. Lincoln did not back down. He held his own, proving he was a brave and strong man, too. Jack and the gang were loyal to Lincoln from that day on.

Around young, single women, Lincoln was shy. But he became a favorite among married women. Perhaps he was able to be himself around them because they were not potential partners. Jack Armstrong's wife, Hannah, had a soft spot for Lincoln, often fixing him a warm meal or mending his torn pants. And Lincoln happily took advice from Graham's wife when he needed it. But there was one young

woman Lincoln became close to. Ann was James Rutledge's daughter, and Abraham got to know her quite well when he roomed at the Rutledge Tavern. Historians disagree if

Lincoln was in love with Ann, but he did go into a depression when she died in 1835.

In March 1832, James Rutledge encouraged Lincoln to run for state legislature. Lincoln was popular, clever, and had experience navigating the river. The success of New Salem was tied to the river. If enough steamboat traffic passed their way, the village would prosper. Abraham joined the Whig Party and began to campaign. His main goals were improving the river to increase traffic and gaining a positive reputation as a politician.

Two things then changed the course of Lincoln's path. Offutt's business failed, leaving him with no job. And the Black Hawk War broke out.

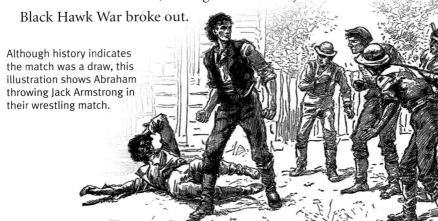

Although history indicates the match was a draw, this illustration shows Abraham throwing Jack Armstrong in their wrestling match.

Lincoln and many others rushed to volunteer for service. The men in Lincoln's company chose him as their captain. They drilled and marched but never saw any action. Still, Lincoln was proud of his first brush with leadership. And he had gained fiercely loyal friends in the process.

Lincoln returned to New Salem just two weeks before the election in August. With little time to campaign, he visited as many voters as he could. Lincoln was in his element, combining his intellectual ideas with his social skills. Still, he lost. With no job and no political office, Lincoln needed a new plan. He became a partner in William Berry's general store. Unfortunately, they were not

good businessmen. Lincoln spent a lot of time reading and talking, while Berry spent a lot of time drinking the store's whiskey. And New Salem was not thriving as all had hoped. Their store failed.

To pay off his debts, Lincoln again turned to odd jobs. Friends came to his aid, too, helping him get two important jobs. He was named postmaster of New Salem in 1833. This let him read all the newspapers in the area—a great benefit for Lincoln. And with Mentor Graham's help,

An idealized image of
Chief Black Hawk.

Black Hawk War

The Black Hawk War was a land dispute. Chief Black Hawk, leading the Sauk and Fox Indians, wanted to resettle on lands in Illinois they believed belonged to them. The U.S. government saw it differently, stating the land had been legally ceded to the government. When Chief Black Hawk led a group of Indians to reclaim the land in April 1832, the Illinois governor saw it as an invasion, causing a war scare among settlers. The governor called out the militia and a war ensued, which ended with Black Hawk's surrender in August.

the county surveyor hired him as his deputy. Lincoln knew nothing about land surveying, but he needed the money and, like the postmaster position, it was good political exposure—more and more people would get to know him. In true Lincoln fashion, he simply set his mind to learning how to do surveying. When Berry died in January 1835, Lincoln took on his debts. It took Lincoln years to pay them off, but he did. This further solidified his reputation as an honest man.

After losing the state legislature race, Lincoln operated this store with William Berry.

chapter 3

Birth of a Politician

Still inexperienced, but ambitious and in need of money, Lincoln ran for state legislature again in 1834. He greeted as many people as he could. He appealed to a wide variety of folks because in addition to being smart, he could farm the fields as well as any other man. He went to every social gathering he could find—dances, picnics, quilting bees, wrestling matches, and house-raisings. He did not talk much about political goals. This was a clever move because, in his area, townspeople tended to be Whigs and rural people tended to be Democrats. It paid off. On August 4, 1834, Lincoln was elected to the state legislature. Lincoln borrowed money from a wealthy New Salem man, Coleman Smoot, to buy a suit. He then went to the Illinois state capital of the time, Vandalia. It was November 1834, and he was 25 years old. Lincoln listened hard and said little in the legislature at first, learning the ropes.

John Todd Stuart was elected to the legislature at the same time. Stuart had served with Lincoln in the Black Hawk War. He supported Lincoln's campaign even though they were competitors. Stuart had gone to college and was a lawyer in

John Todd Stuart, Lincoln's first law partner.

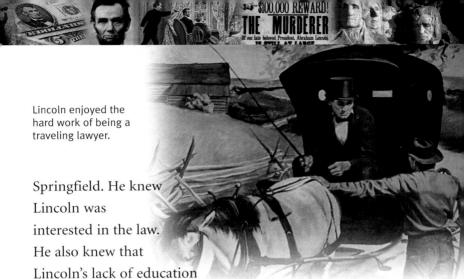

Lincoln enjoyed the hard work of being a traveling lawyer.

Springfield. He knew Lincoln was interested in the law. He also knew that Lincoln's lack of education was a sore spot. Stuart encouraged him to keep studying and loaned him law books. Back in New Salem between legislature sessions, Lincoln studied furiously. As he studied, he formed his own opinions on many subjects, including law, politics, and religion. Sometimes he would get overwhelmed by his thoughts and sink into a depression for a few hours—or a few days.

In 1836, Lincoln was reelected to the legislature. In April 1837, he left New Salem for good and moved to Springfield. It was the newly established capital of Illinois, and Lincoln had worked hard to help pass that decision through the legislature. On March 1, 1837, the self-taught Lincoln was officially licensed to practice law. Stuart hired him as a junior partner in his law firm. This job included being a traveling lawyer for his district, or "riding the circuit" on horseback. Lincoln loved his work, and traveling the circuit gave him exposure to voters in the Springfield area.

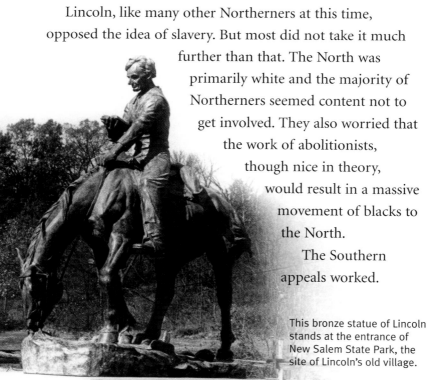

In late 1836, Southern states had begun appealing to governors of northern states—such as Illinois—to squelch the progress of abolitionists. These appeals were largely based on fears of black uprisings, which had begun years earlier. In the 1820s, there were slave unrests in South Carolina. And in 1831, the Nat Turner slave revolt in Virginia sparked tougher slave codes. It also led the South to be further convinced that the work of abolitionists in the North was the cause of slave rebellions.

Lincoln, like many other Northerners at this time, opposed the idea of slavery. But most did not take it much further than that. The North was primarily white and the majority of Northerners seemed content not to get involved. They also worried that the work of abolitionists, though nice in theory, would result in a massive movement of blacks to the North.

The Southern appeals worked.

This bronze statue of Lincoln stands at the entrance of New Salem State Park, the site of Lincoln's old village.

During a session in Vandalia, in January 1837, the Illinois legislature had passed proslavery resolutions stating that owning slaves was a constitutional right and that abolitionist groups were dangerous. Given the opinions of the times, it would not have been surprising if Lincoln had voted in keeping with his peers. But Lincoln voted no. It was his first official statement against slavery. And out of 83 votes, his was only one of six opposed. It was a brave move, because being labeled an abolitionist could have ruined Lincoln's political career.

Nat Turner Rebellion

Nat Turner was a slave known for his intelligence and his religious beliefs. He had a calling to lead slaves to freedom. On August 22, 1831, he rallied a few slaves in Virginia and they began an uprising. Soon their numbers grew to more than 60. Turner's group killed 55 white people. The police stopped them, but Turner escaped. He was found in October and hanged on November 11, 1831. Before his execution, he was interviewed. Turner's last words survive in *The Confessions of Nat Turner*.

In fact, although Lincoln agreed with many abolitionist sentiments, he did not agree with how carried away abolitionists often got. This was in keeping with his stance on many explosive issues. He was against slavery and believed in such things as temperance

Abolitionists

People who actively fought against slavery were called abolitionists. Some were quite extreme in their tactics and sparked fear in people. Most, however, found effective ways to speak out against slavery, rally support for their cause, and even rescue slaves. The Underground Railroad, for example, was a huge network of people who smuggled countless thousands of slaves to freedom. There were many "conductors," including Levi Coffin and Harriet Tubman. William Lloyd Garrison's antislavery newspaper, the *Liberator*, which was started more than 30 years before the Civil War began, railed against slavery and hailed rights for blacks. Frederick Douglass and Sojourner Truth were two brave and famous black abolitionists of this time.

William Lloyd Garrison

Sojourner Truth

(refraining from drinking alcohol), but he didn't extend those beliefs to joining societies devoted to these causes. In his opinion, banding together in a society tended to drive people to passions that brought more harm than good. Yelling at people, trying to force them to see the error of their ways, he felt, was futile. He later said, "A drop of honey catches more flies than a gallon of gall."

In a speech he gave in January 1838, Lincoln made his feelings about mixing emotions and politics clear. He said the nation's "proud fabric of freedom" should not be compromised by "the jealousy, envy, and avarice, incident to our nature." Lincoln later said he preferred to approach

issues, for the most part, with "persuasion, kind unassuming persuasion."

Lincoln knew just how explosive the issue of slavery could get, how it could even incite mob-mentality responses. In November 1837, a group of enraged citizens had killed the editor of an abolitionist newspaper in Alton, Illinois. Lincoln referred to this incident in the January speech, saying how terrible it was to "throw printing presses into rivers, [and] shoot editors." When it came to sensitive topics, Lincoln believed the nation was best served proceeding with "reason, cold, calculating, unimpassioned reason."

The day Lincoln had arrived in Springfield, April 15, 1837, was the same day he met Joshua Speed. Lincoln had lived in mostly backwater towns, so Springfield—even with its dirt roads and smattering of log cabins amid the nicer homes—was more cosmopolitan than any place he had ever lived. He was still a man with little money and few belongings. Speed and Lincoln became fast friends and lived together in Speed's room above the general store run by Speed.

In the evenings, Lincoln, Speed, and other men would

Joshua Speed, at about the time he first met Lincoln.

Although it was a relatively small town in the 1830s, Springfield, Illinois, was the biggest city Lincoln had ever lived in.

gather around the fire at Speed's store and trade stories. Speed and Lincoln belonged to the Whig Party, but, Speed said, at night "…eight or ten choice spirits assembled, without distinction of party." They talked about politics, books, and the comings and goings of people in the town. Lincoln was often the life of the party, telling jokes or reading poems. But he didn't always join the group. Sometimes he went off by himself to read, or sit quietly and think.

People were drawn to Lincoln. Speed said, "…he did not seek company; it sought him…. They came there because they were sure to find Lincoln." Lincoln inspired closeness and generosity in his friends, and reciprocated when he could, but he was intensely private and did not get too emotionally attached to anyone. Speed was the exception. He became the closest friend of Lincoln's life. And although they did not see each other much in later years, they corresponded intimately. After Lincoln's death, Speed said, "He disclosed his whole heart to me."

There was another man in Springfield at the time, with whom Lincoln had quite a different relationship. Stephen A. Douglas was a Democrat who was quickly becoming Lincoln's main political rival. Douglas was an attorney. The two first met in 1834, while both were serving in the legislature. Lincoln and Douglas disagreed strongly on most topics during legislature sessions. The paths of the towering Whig and the short, stocky Democrat would soon be entwined.

Stephen A. Douglas was a challenging opponent for Lincoln.

chapter 4

Meeting Mary

Lincoln enjoyed the camaraderie he found at Speed's, but he had yet to meet a young woman who made him feel at ease. That changed in the winter of 1839. Mary Todd was an unlikely match for Lincoln. He was gawky, rough around the edges, and from a poor frontier background. Although he was a rising politician, he still had many unpolished ways about him.

Elizabeth Edwards, Mary Todd's sister, and Ninian Edwards (bottom), Mary's brother-in-law, did not approve of Lincoln as a match for Mary.

Mary Todd came from a different world. Hers was a wealthy family that kept slaves. The Todds' house was filled with beautiful things, and Mary had been given a good education. She spoke French, and liked clothes and fancy parties. She went to Springfield in October 1839 to live with her sister Elizabeth and brother-in-law Ninian Edwards. At their parties, many men had their eye on Mary, including Stephen Douglas. Ninian said, "Mary could make a bishop forget his prayers." But Mary liked Abraham instantly.

She could see what was special about this awkward man. Mary knew he was destined for greatness.

Although different in many ways, Mary and Abraham shared important things. They had both lost their mothers very young. And they both, in turn, felt somewhat lost in spite of having strong personalities. They both suffered from mood swings. Mary and Abraham shared a deep love of poetry and politics, Mary being

These are the earliest known photographs of Mary (above) and Abraham (below), taken about four years after their wedding. They were precious to Mary.

quite outspoken for a woman of her time. In fact, Henry Clay often came to dinner at her father's house—and Clay was the politician whose views Lincoln most admired. And Abraham and Mary were both from Kentucky.

The two fell in love and Abraham asked Mary to marry him in the winter of 1840. But just a few weeks later he changed his mind. He was afraid and confused by his feelings, and he had always had trouble with close relationships. There is also some evidence that Mary's family was not happy about the engagement, which could have contributed to Lincoln's hesitation. Whatever the reason, breaking off the engagement did not solve Lincoln's problem. He wrote to Stuart, "I am now the most miserable man living. If what I feel were

equally distributed to the whole human family, there would not be one cheerful face on the earth." Friends even worried that Lincoln might kill himself.

About the time Lincoln called off the engagement, Speed moved to Kentucky. Losing his best friend, especially at this time, was a big blow. In August 1841, Lincoln, still in the throes of depression, went to visit Speed. He felt relaxed and at home with the Speed family and

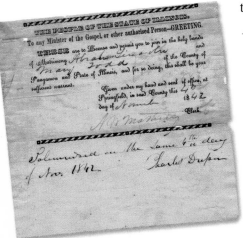

Lincoln had doubts about marrying, but he finally got this marriage license and wed Mary.

began to feel better. He was even able to help with Speed's own fears of marrying the woman *he* loved. Considerably cheered, Lincoln returned to Springfield.

Mary had sent Lincoln a letter to let him know her feelings hadn't changed and that she would "hold the question an open one." Indeed, she had been waiting for him for more than a year. Back in Springfield a mutual friend, Mrs. Simeon Francis, arranged for the couple to meet, and they quietly began to court again.

On the night of November 4, 1842, rain fell against the windowpanes. But inside the Edwards house, Abraham and Mary were married by the light of beautiful oil lamps and a cozy fire. Lincoln was 33 years old. His bride was 10 years younger.

Nine months later, on August 1, 1843, their first son was born. They named him Robert Todd. For a while, the family rented one room at the Globe Tavern. Then, in January 1844, Lincoln bought a house on the corner of Eighth and Jackson streets. They would live there for 17 years.

The Lincoln home in Springfield, Illinois. This photo was taken after the second floor was added in the 1850s.

chapter **5**

Family and Politics

Lincoln was reelected to the Illinois legislature two more times. He learned a lot during his four terms, became skilled at politics, and earned a solid reputation as an intelligent and honest man. In May 1841, Lincoln and John Todd Stuart—who were both spending a lot of time on their political careers—decided to dissolve their partnership. Lincoln became law partners with Stephen Logan. Always the student, the already accomplished Lincoln became an even better attorney from watching Logan and continuing to read. Lincoln said, "When I have a particular case in hand, I love to dig up the question by the roots and hold it up and dry it before the fires of the mind."

This view of Springfield shows the block where Lincoln's law office was located.

Lincoln thoroughly enjoyed practicing law, bringing his unique personality to the courtroom, and charming jurors with his easy manner of speaking about complicated issues. He was a gifted lawyer and took the responsibility of the job seriously. He wrote, "Persuade our neighbors to compromise whenever you can....As a peacemaker the lawyer has a superior opertunity of being a good man....Never stir up litigation." (Lincoln had great ideas, but he couldn't

Lincoln's second law partner, Stephen Logan.

spell "opportunity.") Logan and Lincoln worked together until December 1844. At that time, Logan wanted to go into business with his son, so they agreed to dissolve the firm.

When Lincoln opened his own firm, he asked William

William H. Herndon, Lincoln's third and final law partner.

H. Herndon to be his junior lawyer. Herndon, whom he called Billy, had studied law with Lincoln and Logan. Some thought it was odd for such a well-respected lawyer as Lincoln to choose such an inexperienced partner. But Lincoln planned on running for Congress, which would require him to be out of town, and he trusted Herndon to run the ship. Plus, he simply liked the well-read young man and found him

39

interesting. Mary and Herndon, on the other hand, did not get along at all.

Lincoln did run for Congress in 1845 and won with a huge majority of votes on August 3, 1846. He was the only Whig elected to Congress from Illinois at a time when the president—James Polk—was a Democrat. The Congressional session did not convene until December 6, 1847. In the meantime, Lincoln worked at his law practice and spent time with his family. Mary had given birth to their second son, Edward Baker, on March 10, 1846.

Although this picture shows the Mexicans being beaten, the Americans were badly defeated at the Alamo in 1836. This fueled the fire for the Mexican War ten years later.

Soon after they arrived in Washington, the Lincoln family began living at a boardinghouse near the Capitol building where other Congressmen were also staying. The family of four shared one room. The boys were loud and a bit wild, which did not go over well with the other boarders. With her husband working much of the time, and her having the boys constantly in tow, it didn't take long for Mary to want to leave. By springtime, she had packed up the boys and gone to her father's house in Kentucky.

Mexican War

The Mexican War began in the summer of 1846. Texas had been annexed—taken over—by the United States in 1845, and the boundary at the Rio Grande was under dispute. As the American army fought over that land, it also moved to expand its territory in New Mexico and California. The peace treaty of May 30, 1848, settled the Texas dispute and gave what became New Mexico, Arizona, Colorado, Nevada, Utah, and California to the United States. Still at issue was whether slavery would be allowed to expand into the newly acquired territories.

On his own with no distractions (although his letters show how much he missed Mary and the boys), Lincoln worked tirelessly as a congressman. He served on committees, pushed the need for internal improvements, and tried to introduce a bill that—if it had passed—would have outlawed slavery in Washington, D.C. Lincoln's antislavery views were growing stronger as he witnessed the slave markets in Washington on a frequent basis.

The Mexican War had also offered Lincoln a platform on

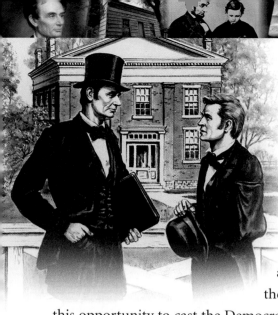

Lincoln continued to be a working lawyer while pursuing his political career. Here, he talks with a client after court.

which to speak. As the war was coming to an end, President Polk stated that Mexico had started the war. Lincoln and other members of the Whig Party leaped at this opportunity to cast the Democrats in a bad light and weaken their chances in the next presidential election. Lincoln gave a fiery speech that pointed the finger at the president, and hence the American army, as being responsible for making the first move toward war. To Lincoln's disappointment, his speech was mostly ignored in Washington. And in Springfield, his views on the Mexican War were met with criticism from Democrats, as well as some Whigs.

After his two-year term in Congress was over in 1849, Lincoln and his family moved back to Springfield. He took a break from politics and concentrated on his law practice. In his autobiography Lincoln wrote, "From 1849 to 1854, both inclusive, [I] practiced law more assiduously than ever before." He and Herndon soon moved into larger office space. But things at home took a dark turn.

Compromise of 1850

As the country expanded, whether or not slavery would be allowed in newly acquired territory was a major issue. Balancing the number of slave and free states had been addressed in 1820 with the Missouri Compromise. In 1850, it was raised by the results of the Mexican War. There was real concern that if laws were passed to keep slavery out of new territories, Southern states would leave the Union. The Compromise of 1850 tried to prevent that. California was admitted as a free state and the other new territories were left to decide on their own at a later date whether they would be slave states or free. Also, the Fugitive Slave Act required citizens to turn in slaves who had escaped their masters. This was especially damaging in the North, where many slaves had begun new lives. Even free blacks were captured. This fired up abolitionists. It also angered many Northerners who had not necessarily paid much attention before. Although the compromise kept the Union together for a while, it brought the issue of slavery ever more into the spotlight.

Little Eddie, not yet four years old, became sick. His parents cared for him night and day for almost two months. On February 1, 1850, he died, most likely from tuberculosis. Abraham and Mary were devastated, and Mary shut herself in her bedroom and cried for weeks. Somehow Lincoln found a way to fight off sinking into a major depression over the loss of his son. He put his energies into his work and caring for Mary, who had begun to act erratically. When she was in good spirits she was a wonderful hostess, but she could also fly into a rage at the slightest provocation. On occasion, if Mary had a

TUBERCULOSIS

Tuberculosis is an infectious disease caused by bacteria that can affect any of the body's organs, especially the lungs.

43

terrible outburst, Lincoln would simply leave the house until she had calmed down.

What helped ease Mary's pain was the birth of their third son, ten months after Eddie died. William Wallace was born on December 21, 1850. Just a few weeks later, on January 17, 1851, Lincoln's father died. He did not travel to the funeral, although he did worry about his stepmother's future. To protect her interests, Lincoln sent a letter to his stepbrother, John Johnston, to make sure that Sally kept enough land to live on.

On April 4, 1853, a fourth son was born to the Lincolns. They named him Thomas, after Abraham's father. The boy's nickname was Tad, short for tadpole, as the boy had an unusually large head! Lincoln took to carrying Tad and Willie with him all over town.

Lincoln was a self-sufficient man who found satisfaction in things such as taking care

Willie was a thoughtful boy who had a strong bond with his father.

of the cow and horse he kept in the backyard. He enjoyed being with his children. And at a time

Tad was bright, outgoing, and quick to play pranks.

when most parents were quite strict with children, the Lincolns were extremely permissive, especially after Eddie's death. Herndon complained about the way in which the Lincoln boys would roam the law office, saying they would "take down the books—empty ash buckets—coal ashes—inkstands—papers—gold pens—letters, etc., etc. in a pile and then dance on the pile."

Also unlike most men of the day, Lincoln played a big role in helping to raise his small children. This was so unusual that it drew comments from townspeople. He spent a lot of time playing with Willie and Tad. He read to them, gave them rides on his shoulders, and towed them around in a toy wagon. Tad had a lisp and a spontaneous nature that was endearing. And Lincoln and Willie shared a common way of thinking. Lincoln said, "I know every step of the process by which that boy arrived at his satisfactory

Lincoln made this working toy wagon for his son Tad.

solution of the question before him, as it is by just such slow methods I attain results."

45

But Lincoln and Robert, his eldest, were not close in the same way that he was to the younger boys. Perhaps it was because Lincoln was away so much when Robert was little.

Unlike when Robert was small, during this time Lincoln was only away from home when he was out riding the circuit. Herndon stayed behind and took care of the office. As neither man was organized, their law office was always a mess, and papers were often lost. They even had a pile on a desk with a string wrapped around it and a note attached that said, "When you can't find it anywhere else, look in this." Herndon and Lincoln had quite different personalities. But they were good at what they did and it was a partnership that worked. Their practice thrived.

Living conditions were usually pretty dismal on the circuit, but Lincoln didn't mind. He enjoyed riding the circuit. It gave him time to be alone, as well as time to socialize with other men. Perhaps it reminded him of the days at Joshua Speed's general store. It was not uncommon for Lincoln, while traveling, to find himself surrounded by a group of men who were happy to listen to him tell stories and jokes. Herndon said, "No one's laugh was heartier than his."

The circuit also gave Lincoln a break from his marriage. It was a complicated relationship, made up of two people who loved each other and who had very different temperaments. Abraham did not show Mary much affection and continued to be plagued with bouts of melancholy. And Mary was

increasingly high strung, hot tempered at times, and frequently annoyed with the shabby way her husband dressed and his unrefined ways.

Lincoln wrote more poetry during this chapter of his life. Some of his words seemed to reflect a certain amount of healing from past emotional wounds. When he visited his boyhood home in Indiana some fifteen years after leaving it, he penned a poem that began:

My childhood's home I see again,
And sadden with the view;
And still, as memory
*   crowds my brain,*
There's pleasure in
*   it too.*

This picture is of the president and his wife shortly after they moved into the White House.

chapter 6

Between Right and Wrong

The Compromise of 1850 was just one event that illuminated the growing differences between the North and the South. As time went on, the division between North and South grew on several fronts. They were becoming more and more economically different from each other, as well as politically opposed.

The North was quickly developing into an industrialized society. Most of the innovations to improve transportation or industrial production had been invented by Northerners. The population in the North grew more rapidly and most of the large cities were there. Workers were needed. The immigrants who came from Europe and other countries

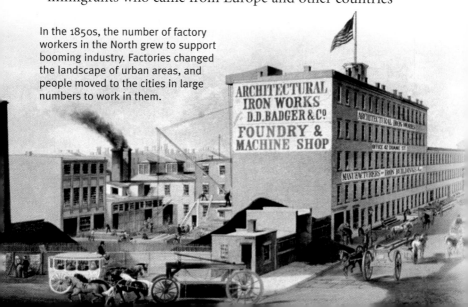

In the 1850s, the number of factory workers in the North grew to support booming industry. Factories changed the landscape of urban areas, and people moved to the cities in large numbers to work in them.

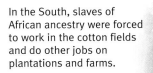

In the South, slaves of African ancestry were forced to work in the cotton fields and do other jobs on plantations and farms.

settled mainly in the North. There they could find jobs working in factories and building roads, bridges, railroads, and other improvements. The South, on the other hand, was mainly agricultural. Only a tenth of the nation's goods were being manufactured in the South. The economy of the South relied heavily on growing crops such as cotton. Supplying the cotton, in turn, relied heavily on the plantation system and slavery.

As the Northern states grew economically and industrially, having a stronger centralized government made sense. This would provide the support needed for continued growth. Business was no longer conducted just locally. Roads and railroads, which linked states to one another, facilitated trade on a larger basis. Plus the nation now had a single federal currency. These advancements depended upon government support. The Southern states, on the other hand, still felt comfortable being sovereign states and governing themselves.

SOVEREIGN STATE

A sovereign state governs itself and does not consider itself subject to the rule of the federal government.

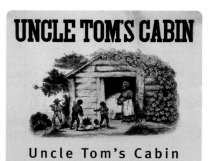

UNCLE TOM'S CABIN

Uncle Tom's Cabin

A year after the Compromise of 1850, Harriet Beecher Stowe's antislavery novel, *Uncle Tom's Cabin*, started to shake people up. It rallied more antislavery supporters in the North and angered many people in the South, further separating the nation. When Lincoln later met Stowe in 1862, he affectionately called her the "little lady who made this big war."

They didn't feel they had much to gain from a more powerful federal government. On the contrary, Southerners felt that a strong government would mean the end of slavery—and their prosperity.

And, of course, the biggest issue pitting North against South was slavery. An important point to keep in mind is that, for many politicians, including Lincoln, the goal in the 1850s was not to abolish slavery; it was to preserve the Union. But since it was the main issue dividing the Union, slavery became the primary focus.

About a year after little Tad was born, something happened to pull Lincoln sharply back into the world of politics. In 1820, the Missouri Compromise had made slavery illegal in the region that, in 1854, was on the verge of becoming Kansas and Nebraska. Lincoln's old rival Stephen A. Douglas, now a senator, passed the Kansas-Nebraska Act

in May 1854. The act overturned the effect of the compromise in those territories, making slavery legal. Douglas maintained that he was not advocating slavery, simply the right of sovereign territories to make their own decisions. Abolitionists were outraged.

Lincoln was "thunderstruck." Douglas's act urged him on "as he had never been aroused before." Lincoln had long held the belief that slavery would die out on its own, but the Kansas-Nebraska Act threatened that belief. He said, "It is wrong, wrong in its…effect, letting slavery into Kansas and Nebraska—and wrong in…principle, allowing it to spread to every other part of the wide world…"

Both the Democrat and Whig parties suffered from having split feelings regarding slavery. The Democrats lost many members. The Whigs began to fall apart entirely, unable to agree on their platforms any longer. Lincoln remained loyal to the Whigs for as long as he felt able, but he ultimately left the crumbling party. From disillusioned Democrats, Whigs, and others, the Republican Party was born. It was united in the belief that slavery should not be allowed to expand. Because Republicans were sympathetic to the cause of ending slavery, their enemies sometimes called them the Black Republicans. Lincoln joined this new group in 1856. That same year, the Republicans put forth their first presidential candidate, John Fremont, who lost.

The fallout from the Kansas-Nebraska Act was not just political. Geographically, Nebraska was not an immediate

Mary renovated their home—on the inside and the outside. Abraham did not share her lavish and expensive sense of style.

hotbed. But Kansas was vulnerable because it shared a border with Missouri, a slave state. In May 1856, a group of proslavery men burned down a hotel in Lawrence, Kansas, and destroyed several homes and stores. A few days later, abolitionist John Brown was responsible for the killings of five other proslavery men. For four months, the opposing groups lashed out at each other in what was called "Bloody Kansas." There were even violent outbursts in Congress. The Southern—and abolitionist—Senator Charles Sumner gave a speech condemning proslavery senators. In response, Congressman Preston Brooks attacked Sumner right at his desk, beating him with a cane!

To fight for what he held true, Lincoln decided to run for the Senate. In part because of the splintering of the parties, he lost his first time out, in 1855. But he won the Republican Party nomination in 1858. In the meantime, he continued to devote his time to his law practice and his family. Mary was in better spirits these days, with her husband home more and making a respectable income. She even had the chance to

renovate their house and entertain guests, two things that made her quite happy. In fact, she threw a birthday party for Lincoln in 1857 and invited 500 guests!

At the time the Lincolns bought their house it was one-and-a-half stories. When the workers were finished, it was a two-story home with plenty of space for their family. Lincoln teased Mary, saying to a neighbor, "Stranger, do you know where Lincoln lives? He used to live here." Indeed, Mary's taste in draperies, carpeting, wallpapers, and furnishings added up to a costly remodeling project that was a sign of things to come when she later took on the White House.

Meanwhile, the political battle over slavery did not showing any signs of cooling down. In the Dred Scott Decision of 1857, the Supreme Court ruled that blacks were not citizens, were not included in the "all men are created equal" part of the Declaration of Independence, and had no right to sue. This court

Dred Scott Decision

Dred Scott was a slave whose master took him out of Missouri and into free territory. In 1846, Scott sued for his freedom based on this fact. More than 10 years later, Supreme Court Justice Roger B. Taney ruled that blacks could not sue and that Dred Scott was a slave regardless of where he lived.

53

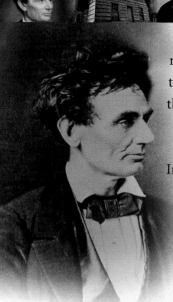

ruling increased antislavery feelings in the North, giving Republicans a boost in the next election. Lincoln spoke out, saying that if things kept going in this direction the Declaration of Independence would become "assailed, and sneered at, and construed, and hawked at, and torn, till, if its framers could rise from their graves, they could not at all recognize it."

This is the second known photograph of Lincoln and is often called the "tousled-hair" portrait. Before Alexander Hesler took the photo, he tried to tame Lincoln's unruly hair by pushing it off his forehead.

On June 16, 1858, Lincoln gave a speech acknowledging his party's nomination to run against Douglas in the upcoming Senate election. He said, "A house divided against itself cannot stand. I believe this government cannot endure, permanently half slave and half free....It will become all one thing, or all the other." Lincoln used this theme of a house divided, which came from the Bible as well as his beloved childhood *Aesop's Fables*, for a specific reason. He wanted to make sure people knew that his opponent, Douglas, was in favor of the expansion of slavery and should not be trusted with the preservation of the Union.

As much as Lincoln heartily distrusted Douglas, Douglas respected the Illinois Republican and knew he was in for a good fight. "I shall have my hands full....He is the strong man of his party—full of wit, facts, dates, and the best stump-speaker, with his droll ways and dry jokes, in the West. He is as honest as he is shrewd; and if I beat him, my victory will be hardly won," Douglas said.

Lincoln asked Douglas to engage in a series of debates with him. From August to October, the two rivals faced off seven times. Crowds of thousands came on foot, on horseback, in buggies, on trains, and on boats to hear them. You could smell the smoke of thundering cannon, hear the drums beat and the horns blare as bands and fireworks added to the drama. The two men were opposite in every way. Douglas was known throughout the country; Lincoln had mainly a local reputation. The thin, towering Lincoln dwarfed the small, stocky Douglas, nicknamed the "Little Giant." Douglas would stomp his foot or wave his fist and had a booming, dramatic voice. Lincoln was stiff and made odd movements, and his voice often became high-pitched. Douglas wore fancy clothes, and Lincoln

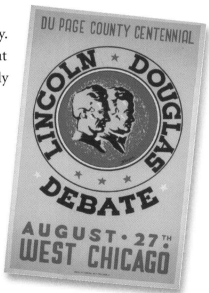

The Lincoln-Douglas debates were so important they are often reenacted. This poster is from one such reenactment.

chose plain. He wanted voters to know he was one of them. In each debate, the opening speaker had an hour to talk. The man who followed was given an hour and a half to reply, and then the first speaker wrapped it up in the last 30 minutes.

It is tempting to think that things were clear-cut back then, but they were not. Even though he opposed slavery, like most people of his day, Lincoln did think that whites were superior to blacks. At the debate in Charleston Lincoln said, "I am not, nor ever have been in favor of bringing about in any way the social and political equality of the white and black races…there must be the position of superior and inferior, and I as much as any other man am in favor of having the superior position assigned to the white race."

Famous photographer Mathew Brady shot this picture of Lincoln when he traveled to New York City to give his Cooper Union address. He is wearing his new black suit.

But this view did not keep Lincoln from believing that slavery was wrong, and it did not keep him from believing that the forefathers meant "all men" when they wrote "all men." The debates marked the time in Lincoln's career when he came out strongly against the morality of slavery. At the first debate, Lincoln charged that Douglas was "blowing out the moral lights around us." At the last one, he said, "The real issue in this controversy…is the sentiment on the part of one class that looks upon the institution of slavery as a wrong, and of another class that does not…It is the eternal struggle between these two principles—right and wrong.…"

Lincoln was the underdog in this race for the Senate. He had worked hard for every political success he had achieved so far, while Douglas was enjoying an easy rise in politics. Lincoln lost the election in November, but he won fame and the opportunity to reach multitudes of people. Even though he was gloomy from defeat, he said, "I believe I have made some marks which will tell for the cause of civil liberty long after I am gone."

Lincoln was afraid his political career was over. Referring to his partner Herndon, he remarked, "I expect everyone to desert me except Billy." But his fears were unfounded. He was now regarded as a solid leader of the Republican Party. Lincoln was invited to share his views at the Cooper Union hall in New York City on February 27, 1860. He bought a new black suit for the occasion and had famed photographer Mathew Brady take his portrait during his visit.

As always, Lincoln's delivery was peppered with his backwoods Kentucky pronunciations, saying things like "cheermun" instead of "chairman." His manner took many

John Brown and Harpers Ferry

On October 16, 1859, abolitionist John Brown led another attack, this time on Harpers Ferry in northern Virginia. His goal was to start a slave rebellion. He didn't succeed, but it fueled the fire of Southern alarm about antislavery activities.

people in the sophisticated crowd by surprise. But he quickly won them over with the power of his words. In his speech, he talked about how Southerners should not confuse the wild abolitionist activities of John Brown with the moral antislavery platform of the Republican Party.

As before, he appealed to reason, not rising tempers, and pointed out the complexities of the issue. "Wrong as we think slavery is, we can yet afford to let it alone where it is…but can we, while our votes will prevent it, allow it to spread into the National Territories, and to overrun us here in these Free States?…Let us have faith that right makes might, and in that faith, let us, to the end, dare to do our duty as we understand it." When he was done, the crowd leaped to its feet, clapping and cheering. The newspapers gave him glowing reviews.

Before returning to Illinois, Lincoln visited his son Robert

at school in New Hampshire and made more speeches in New England. During the Senate campaign, Lincoln had laughed at Mary's idea that he would one day be president. He commented to a reporter, "Just think of such a sucker as me as president." But his confidence was growing. When he got back from New York he wrote, "The taste *is* in my mouth a little."

That year, the Republican National Convention was in Chicago. On May 18, 1860, Lincoln was in Springfield, waiting to hear if he was his party's candidate for president. He was restless and didn't think he would win. He even went outside to play "fives" handball to pass the time. But when the news came, it was good. Springfield fired off a 100-gun salute and a crowd gathered outside the Lincoln home to cheer him on.

People gather at Lincoln's Springfield home in August 1860 to support their Republican presidential candidate. Willie is watching from upstairs.

Willie Lincoln   Abraham Lincoln

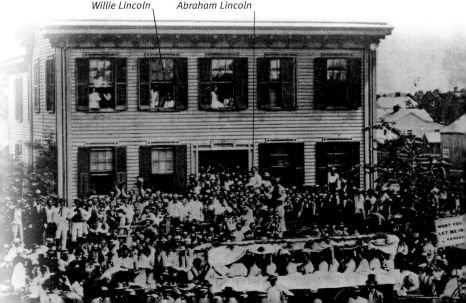

chapter 7

Preparing for Washington

People flocked to meet the presidential candidate. Lincoln took an office in the state capitol building and worked there throughout the summer. He was swamped with preparations for the campaign. There were letters to answer, requests for interviews, people who wanted to photograph him, and countless other tasks. Lincoln hired John Nicolay as his personal secretary.

Lincoln's campaign, in part, took on a life of its own. In the North, he was characterized as the down-home, rail-splitting Honest Abe. In the South, he was so hated that his name didn't even appear on the ballot.

Lincoln had three opponents in the election. The Democrats, now divided, had chosen two candidates—Douglas and John C. Breckinridge. A fourth candidate, John Bell, was put

Lincoln with his secretaries—John Nicolay (seated) and John Hay. They opened a few hundred letters a day and fielded all types of requests made of the president.

forth by the Constitutional Union Party. With no formal education and no real experience administrating a government, Lincoln won the presidential election in November—without one vote from the South. The South was furious. The *Dallas Herald* wrote, "The evil days…are upon us." The *Augusta Constitutionalist* ominously reported, "The South should arm at once."

Lincoln replied in writing to Grace Bedell's request that he grow a beard. It is said that Lincoln kept her letter and often showed it to people.

Meanwhile, Mary was enjoying the excitement and prospect of becoming first lady, and she wanted a new wardrobe. She went on the first of what would become many troublesome shopping sprees in New York. Lincoln stayed in Springfield and continued his work, hiring another secretary, John Hay, to deal with the increased load. One of the people who wrote to him at this time was an 11-year-old girl named Grace Bedell. She thought Lincoln would look more appealing if he grew a beard. It appears he took Grace's advice.

Less than two weeks before moving to Washington, Lincoln visited his stepmother and said a tearful good-bye.

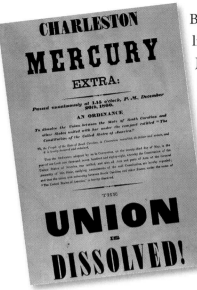

CHARLESTON

MERCURY

EXTRA:

Passed unanimously at 1.15 o'clock, P.M., December 20th, 1860.

AN ORDINANCE

To dissolve the Union between the State of South Carolina and other States united with her under the compact entitled "The Constitution of the United States of America."

We, the People of the State of South Carolina, in Convention assembled, do declare and ordain, and it is hereby declared and ordained,

That the Ordinance adopted by us in Convention, on the twenty-third day of May, in the year of our Lord one thousand seven hundred and eighty-eight, whereby the Constitution of the United States of America, was ratified, and also, all Acts and parts of Acts of the General Assembly of this State, ratifying amendments of the said Constitution, are hereby repealed; and that the union now subsisting between South Carolina and other States, under the name of "The United States of America," is hereby dissolved.

THE

UNION

IS

DISSOLVED!

The news of South Carolina's secession was declared with this announcement in the *Charleston Mercury*.

Back in Springfield, he gave his little dog Fido to a boy named Johnny Roll and his horse, Old Bob, to other neighbors. The Lincolns rented out their house. The soon-to-be president and first lady packed up their belongings in trunks and labeled them "A. Lincoln, The White House."

It was raining on the morning of February 11, 1861, but people gathered at the train station to say good-bye to Lincoln and his family. Along with Nicolay, Hay, and others was Ward Hill Lamon. Lamon was a lawyer friend of Lincoln's, whose rowdy company he enjoyed. Lamon was devoted to Lincoln and came on as his bodyguard. Most of the trip was exciting, as throngs of people waved and cheered. The train stopped several times so the next president could speak to the crowds. In Westfield, New York, he even met little Grace Bedell, pulling her up onto the platform to give her a kiss.

But trouble had been brewing since the announcement of Lincoln's election in November. South Carolina was the first state to secede—or separate—from the Union, in December 1860.

On January 9, 1861, Mississippi seceded. Florida was next on January 10, and Alabama seceded the next day. Southern states seized many federal forts in the South. By February 4, before Lincoln had even boarded the train to Washington, D.C., Georgia, Louisiana, and Texas had all left the United States. On February 9, Jefferson Davis became president of the newly formed Confederate States of America. Between April and June, four more states would join the Confederacy. The South was determined to preserve slavery. And Lincoln, at first believing secessionists were led by a small group of wealthy men, may have underestimated how serious the nation's situation was.

When Lincoln's train got to Philadelphia, the travelers learned of an assassination plot that was to take place in Baltimore. Not knowing whether it was a real threat or not, but advised to play it safe, Lamon and Lincoln secretly got off the train before Baltimore. A felt hat replaced his usual stovepipe hat, disguising Lincoln. He arrived safely in Washington, but was ridiculed for sneaking into town. Lincoln remained uncomfortable about the whole episode, but felt he did the best he could with the information he had at the time.

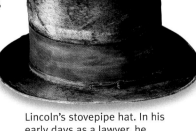

Lincoln's stovepipe hat. In his early days as a lawyer, he sometimes stuck legal papers in his hat so as not to lose them.

63

chapter 8

Begins with a Bang!

A crowd huddles in front of the Capitol Building, clutching their coats to keep out the wind while they wait. Sharpshooters line the rooftops, on the lookout for assassins. Soldiers block traffic. It is March 4, 1861. Vice President Hannibal Hamlin has just been sworn in. And Lincoln is about to deliver his inaugural address. Douglas, despite having been defeated, stands nearby, graciously holding his old rival's tall stovepipe hat during the ceremony.

Lincoln's speech had been carefully crafted. He needed to make his position known while appealing to Southerners. He strove to avoid a civil war—war between citizens of the same nation—over the issue of slavery and urged the seceded states to rejoin the Union. Lincoln wrote the speech, but asked advisors for changes that might help avoid stirring Southern

The Capitol Building was not yet finished on the day of Lincoln's inauguration.

tempers. The time had come to speak. Lincoln said, "Before entering upon so grave a matter as the destruction of our national fabric, with all its benefits, its memories and its hopes, would it not be wise to ascertain precisely why we do it? In your hands, my dissatisfied fellow countrymen, and not in mine, is the momentous issue of civil war. The government will not assail you. You can have no conflict, without being yourselves the aggressors. You have no oath registered in Heaven to destroy the government, while I shall have the most solemn one to 'preserve, protect and defend' it.

Jefferson Davis

A few weeks before Lincoln's inauguration, Jefferson Davis, who was in favor of the expansion of slavery, was elected president of the newly formed Confederate States of America. The structure of the C.S.A.'s government was much the same as the one the seven states had seceded from, as was the Confederate Constitution that was drawn up— with one major difference: the right to own slaves was clearly stated. Davis was sworn in as president on February 18, 1861.

"I am loth [sic] to close. We are not enemies, but friends. We must not be enemies. Though passion may have strained, it must not break our bonds of affection. The mystic chords of memory, stretching from every battlefield, and patriot grave, to every living heart and hearthstone, all over this broad land, will yet swell the chorus of the Union, when again touched, as surely they will be, by the better angels of our nature."

But the "better angels of our nature" were not ready to emerge. The following morning Lincoln got word that Fort Sumter, in South Carolina, was surrounded by the Confederacy and running out of supplies. William Seward, the secretary of state, advised Lincoln to abandon the fort, but he would not. If he sent supplies, the Confederacy was likely to attack. If he didn't, the fort would not be able to hold out.

Lincoln did not make quick decisions, especially when the stakes were so high. The American flag flying above Fort Sumter was a symbol he did not want to see taken down. Lincoln rallied opinions from the more experienced politicians around him. A fact-finding mission to South Carolina brought back news that reinforcing Fort Sumter would be seen as an act of war.

By March 29, Lincoln was deeply discouraged. The fate of the Union was in his hands, and time was running out. He made his decision. On April 6, word was sent to

The bombardment of Fort Sumter on April 12, 1860, marked the start of the Civil War.

the governor of South Carolina that provisions were being sent "and that, if such attempt be not resisted, no effort to throw in men, arms, or ammunition, will be made…" Lincoln made it clear he was doing his best to avoid a conflict.

The provision ships had not yet arrived. But upon hearing the news from the governor, Jefferson Davis demanded the surrender of Fort Sumter. In command of the fort, Major Robert Anderson refused. Confederate forces opened fire on April 12 at 4:30 AM. The Civil War had begun.

Southerners in favor of states' rights rushed to join the Confederate Army.

On April 14, Fort Sumter surrendered. The next day, Lincoln issued a proclamation calling for 75,000 militia volunteers. Men rushed to join, singing and cheering against the South. In the South, young men railed against the North just the same. Many Southern soldiers did not care as much about slavery as they did about a state's right to decide for itself. Two sides of one nation were fueled by fury. Virginia seceded, and the Confederacy set up its own capital. Within the next

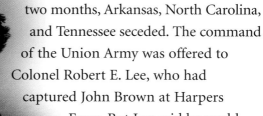

two months, Arkansas, North Carolina, and Tennessee seceded. The command of the Union Army was offered to Colonel Robert E. Lee, who had captured John Brown at Harpers Ferry. But Lee said he could not fight against his fellow Virginians and Southerners. Although Lee opposed slavery, he joined the Confederacy and took command of the Virginia state troops.

To create a military image, an artist added his vision of a Confederate general's uniform to a civilian photo of Robert E. Lee.

Washington, D.C., was bordered by Virginia and nearly surrounded by the slave state of Maryland. A riot had broken out in Baltimore and tempers were flaring. It felt to many that D.C. was surrounded by enemies and there were no Union troops yet in sight. With a telescope, Lincoln could see Confederate campfires and tents in the distance. Things were getting dangerous. Then, on April 25, Union troops began marching into the capital, and soon it was teeming with soldiers. Lincoln was relieved.

With the goal of preserving the Union clearly before him, Lincoln dug in. He blockaded Confederate ports with Union ships. He called for more volunteers and added regiments to the army. And, to allow for the arrest of rebel sympathizers, he suspended the writ of habeas corpus.

Lincoln believed secession was not legal. Therefore, the Confederacy was not legal and the Southern states were, in actuality, still part of the Union. As president, it was his job to put down the rebellion and repair the Union. In July 1861, Lincoln called a special session of Congress to explain what he saw as the big picture—that this was a fight to save democracy. He said, "It presents to the whole family of man, the question, whether a constitutional republic, or a democracy—a government of the people, by the same people—can, or cannot, maintain its territorial integrity, against its own domestic foes.... On the side of the Union, it is a struggle for maintaining in the world, that form, and substance of government, whose leading object is, to elevate the condition of men…to afford all, an unfettered start, and a fair chance, in the race of life." The speech won over many who had doubted him.

Lincoln also needed to keep the peace with the border states—Kentucky, Missouri, Delaware, and Maryland. This meant making sure these slave states understood Lincoln's stance on slavery as it pertained to the war. Although personally opposed, he did not believe it was Constitutional to interfere in a state's right to hold slaves. He did not want slavery to expand, but he did not intend to interfere with slavery that already existed.

The first major battle of the Civil War took place on

BORDER STATES

Border states were Southern slave states that bordered northern free states and did not secede from the Union.

July 21, 1861, at a creek called Bull Run in Virginia. Many Northerners had been confident that the war would be short. But the defeat of Union troops by the Confederacy showed that there would be no quick and easy victory. Lincoln did not sleep that night as he learned of the details of the battle. More than 600 soldiers had been killed. The next day, he put George B. McClellan in charge of troops near the capital, naming him Commander of the Army of the Potomac.

On August 6, 1861, Lincoln signed the First Confiscation Act. This stated that slaves used by the Confederacy for military purposes could be confiscated and freed. Lincoln did this at a time when there was a severe lack of action on the war front. After Bull Run, McClellan had not moved the troops into battle. He tried to shift responsibility for this to his superior, 75-year-old General Winfield Scott. When Scott resigned on November 1, Lincoln made McClellan general-in-chief. An overconfident McClellan told the president, "I can do it all." But by January,

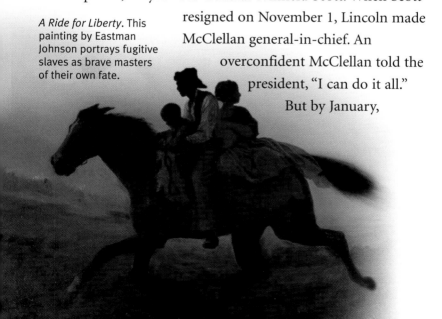

A Ride for Liberty. This painting by Eastman Johnson portrays fugitive slaves as brave masters of their own fate.

McClellan had still not moved into action. People were
starting to think that, although honest and well intended,
Lincoln might not be up to the job. He couldn't get his top
general to fight! Lincoln took steps to strengthen the war
department. He replaced the ineffective Secretary of War
Simon Cameron with Edwin M. Stanton. The following
month, General Ulysses S. Grant quickly moved his Union
troops and took two Confederate forts—Fort Henry and
Fort Donelson. And by early 1862, beginning with Kentucky,
all four border states had sided with the Union. Things
were looking up.

But Lincoln was having a difficult time at home. He
worked without stopping, and it put a strain on him and
Mary. She needed him to help calm her nerves, but he was
not available. Mary and Abraham used to enjoy discussing
politics together, but he no longer had time. While her
husband concentrated on things outside the White House,
Mary concentrated on the inside. She went on shopping
sprees, buying clothes, glassware, furniture, wallpaper, and
draperies. Lincoln had suggested the idea. But her spending
got out of hand. Congress had allotted $20,000 to be spent
over four years, and Mary spent much more than that just
during the summer of 1861.

Mary tried to hide her overspending from her husband.
When Lincoln found out about it, he was angry. "It would
stink in the land to have it said that an appropriation of
$20,000 for furnishing the house had been overrun by the

President when the poor freezing soldiers could not have blankets." Mary, on the other hand, thought the White House should reflect a symbol of the strong and splendid Union. They quarreled.

The Lincolns did not fight, however, about their children. Robert was away at Harvard. But the two younger boys were allowed to run free in the White House. Imagine how exciting it was for them to have soldiers in

This famous photo of Lincoln and Tad was taken by Mathew Brady. It was used as a model for later images that added family members and changed the photo album they are looking at to a book.

their house! The boys kept goats and a pony, played games, and frequently interrupted Cabinet meetings and state dinners. People complained, but it did not bother Lincoln at all. He called them his "blessed fellows." He and Mary both wanted their children to enjoy themselves. Since neither one of them had had happy childhoods, they indulged their children's wishes.

Although Willie and Tad both had great fun, Willie was quieter and more serious than Tad. He was gentle and sweet and liked to read. Lincoln loved to have both his boys around him, but there seemed to be an especially close bond between Lincoln and Willie. Their personalities were similar.

TYPHOID FEVER

Typhoid fever is an infectious disease transmitted by contaminated food or water. Sanitation was much different in the 1860s than it is today. It is likely that the White House water was polluted.

In February 1862, Willie and Tad both became ill. As Willie worsened, Mary did not leave his side. He died of typhoid fever on February 20, 1862. A grieving Lincoln said, "My poor boy, he was too good for this earth…but then we loved him so." Mary could not bear the loss. She did not leave her bed for almost a month. At any other time, Lincoln would likely have sunk into a deep depression, too. But the nation depended upon him. Although he would often think of Willie and cry, he threw himself even further into his work.

As Lincoln gained more experience as commander-in-chief, his comfort level with making war decisions rose. During the Fort Sumter situation, he had turned to his advisors for guidance—many of whom had more experience than he did. But he trusted his instincts even then, and by late 1862, he realized he must look to himself for the answers. In true Lincoln fashion, he started reading up on military strategy to educate himself.

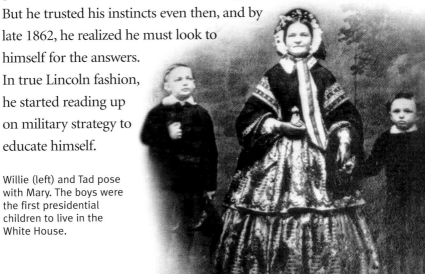

Willie (left) and Tad pose with Mary. The boys were the first presidential children to live in the White House.

chapter 9

Emancipation!

Although long opposed to slavery, Lincoln had focused on restoring the Union, not abolishing slavery. But he began to receive more and more pressure to do something about it. In the meantime, thousands of slaves were making their way North—toward freedom. And although they were risking their lives to head for the Union, more and more slaves did it. Lincoln was also well aware that free blacks in the North may have had their freedom, but they were not treated equally.

On August 14, 1862, Lincoln called a meeting of black leaders to the White House—the first time any such gathering had ever been held there. He wanted to propose an idea. He described the situation, as he saw it, to the men. "Your race are suffering, in my judgment, the greatest wrong inflicted on any people. But even when you cease to be slaves, you are yet far removed from being placed on an equality with the white race....Go where you are treated the best, and the ban is still upon you....I need not recount to you the effects upon white men, growing out of the institution of Slavery....without the institution of Slavery and the colored race as a basis, the war could not have an existence....It is better for us both, therefore, to be separated." Then he laid out a plan for voluntary

recolonization that involved sending blacks to Central America and the Caribbean to live.

Frederick Douglass was insulted and angry. He said Lincoln had "contempt for Negroes" and was "canting hypocrisy." Lincoln's proposal seemed to amount to wishing that blacks—and thus, the nation's problem—would just go away. Lincoln later realized his mistake. In 1864, he sent the navy to bring back the blacks who had been re-colonized.

Meanwhile, the Union was not making progress on the military front. The war was dragging on, thousands of men were dying, and there were no results in sight. Lincoln needed to strike at the heart of the issue—slavery. He began to believe that the preservation of the Union depended, in part, upon the destruction of slavery. But in order for this idea to be accepted by Northerners of

Frederick Douglass

Frederick Douglass was born a slave in Maryland in 1818. After teaching himself to read and write, he read about the antislavery movement in a newspaper when he was 13 years old. He escaped in 1838, and a few years later, in Massachusetts, began speaking out against slavery. In 1845, he published his autobiography and quickly became both well known and well respected. Douglass became the most famous African-American of the 1800s.

The Contraband Relief Association

Elizabeth Keckley was a former slave who worked at the White House as a seamstress. She looked after Mary Lincoln and helped comfort her after Willie died. When Mary finally felt able to face the world again, Keckley encouraged Mary to help her with her newly formed Contraband Relief Association. "Contraband" was the term used for runaway slaves, many of whom were stuck in limbo with nowhere to go and no means to live. Mary turned some of her grief into compassion and helped Elizabeth when she could. She helped Keckley raise money, and even had Lincoln spend $200 on bedding to help provide clean beds for the freed slaves. And she found odd jobs for those she could.

Elizabeth Keckley

many different moral and political views, it needed to be based on the war, not morals or politics. On July 22, 1862, Lincoln had proposed the Emancipation Proclamation—which would free the slaves in the Confederacy—to his Cabinet. Seward believed the Union needed a military victory first, or else risk the proclamation being viewed "as the last measure of an exhausted government, a cry for help." Lincoln agreed to wait.

But the Union armies were not making much progress. And Lincoln's popularity was suffering. In April 1862, Lincoln—frustrated by McClellan's constant stalling—had sent the general a letter telling him to act immediately. But McClellan complained about bad weather and needing reinforcements, and gave other excuses. Leaders of the other sections of Union forces were not gaining ground either. Thousands upon thousands of lives were being lost. May, June, and July proved no better. Lincoln was worried. He grew depressed. He was not eating or sleeping much. He looked worn out and haggard. Determined to be victorious, Lincoln said, "I expect to maintain this contest until successful or till I die, or am conquered, or my term expires, or Congress or the country forsakes me."

Then, on September 17, the new commander of the Confederate Army, the formidable General Robert E. Lee, invaded Northern soil in Maryland at Sharpsburg, near Antietam Creek. Lincoln sent McClellan to stop him. McClellan fought them off and gained ground, but continued to hesitate throughout the battle. Lee's forces were able to retreat.

Lincoln visited McClellan at his headquarters in October 1862, urging him to fight more vigorously.

The losses were huge. More than 12,000 Union soldiers and 10,000 Confederate soldiers lay dead. Confederate soldiers had been driven from Northern soil, but a major opportunity to wipe out Lee's army had passed. While McClellan was overjoyed by his success, Lincoln was disappointed in McClellan's failure to finish off the rebels. Still, Antietam was a victory for the Union—a victory that gave Lincoln the chance he needed to announce his Emancipation Proclamation.

Just five days later, on September 22, Lincoln read it to his

Sioux Uprising

In August 1862, there was a Sioux uprising in Minnesota. The Sioux were not getting what was owed them for giving up their lands. A small group broke into a farm, stole food, and ended up killing five white settlers. The violence spread and more than 350 whites were killed. Minnesota's governor said all 303 Sioux involved should be executed. Lincoln went through the list of crimes and managed to single out 39 instead. December 26, 1862, marked the largest mass execution in U.S. history.

Confederate casualties from the Battle of Antietam.

Cabinet. First he shared a bawdy story with them, as he was feeling lighthearted for the first time in a long while. Many of his Cabinet members did not approve of Lincoln's rough, backwoods way of joking and using rough language. But Lincoln was a man who did not pretend to be something he was not. Being true to his nature endeared him to many.

The Emancipation Proclamation put the focus of the war squarely on the issue of slavery.

Lincoln signed the Emancipation Proclamation on January 1, 1863. It said, in part, "as a fit and necessary war measure...I do order and declare that all persons held as slaves...henceforward shall be free; and that the Executive government of the United States...will recognize and maintain the freedom of said persons." Southerners were outraged. In the North, most Republicans were pleased; most Democrats were not. The document freed only slaves in rebel states, but it was an enormous first step. It changed Lincoln, and it changed the nature of the war. Now it was a war that needed to be won in order to fulfill the promises he had made.

10

Lincoln's War

In November 1862, the war was far from being won. Lincoln had grown weary of McClellan's constant excuses and inability to lead his men into action. There were delays on the other fronts as well. When McClellan wrote that his horses were too "fatigued" to move, Lincoln replied, "Will you pardon me for asking what the horses of your army have done since the battle of Antietam that fatigue anything?" He relieved McClellan of his command and appointed General Ambrose E. Burnside.

The following month, Burnside led his troops through a bloody defeat in the Battle of Fredericksburg, in Virginia. Seemingly unable to find the

A cartoon from a northern newspaper shows the womanly embodiment of America blaming Lincoln for the soldiers lost at the Battle of Fredericksburg. The media of Lincoln's day was often critical of the war effort.

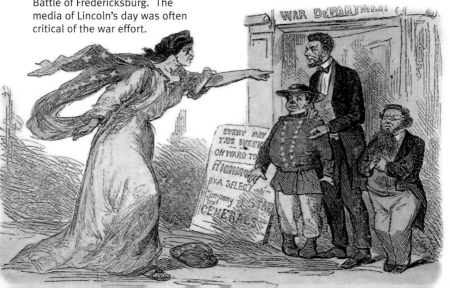

right general to command the Army of the Potomac, Lincoln replaced Burnside with Joseph Hooker, or "Fighting Joe," in January 1863. Wounded and sick men lay in hospital beds. Disillusioned men who did not want to fight a war on slavery deserted. Anti-war sentiment spread, as did anti-Lincoln feelings. People blamed him for the long, bloody war. Unfortunately, his new general, Hooker, also turned out to be a disappointment. In May 1863, Hooker had twice as many soldiers as

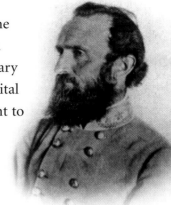

Jackson, standing firm during the first major battle of the Civil War, was given his nickname "Stonewall."

Lee, who split his men with Confederate General Thomas J. "Stonewall" Jackson. Together, the two rebel forces badly

Lincoln and the Soldiers' Home

Beginning in 1862, Lincoln spent summers at a cottage on the grounds of the Soldiers' Home. The horse or carriage ride between the White House and the Soldiers' Home offered him a chance to see what was going on in the streets. The cottage and the lawns offered the family relief from the hot city. And the getaway allowed the president a place to gather his thoughts when needed, hold private meetings, and visit with friends.

defeated Hooker's troops in the Battle of Chancellorsville. Lincoln was distraught. "My god! My god! What will the country say!"

The president was having trouble with his people in the White House, as well. It seemed chaos was all around him. Secretary of the Treasury Salmon Chase was increasingly upset by what he saw as Secretary of State Seward's

81

negative influence on the president. Seward and Lincoln often met alone to discuss issues. Privately, Chase rallied many senators against Seward in the hopes of forcing him out. And it almost worked. When Seward got wind of his disfavor, he offered to resign. But when Lincoln listened to all the complaints, he believed Chase was responsible for the situation. Lincoln invited the senators to a Cabinet meeting during which the truth came out. Chase then offered his resignation. But Lincoln simply wanted the matter resolved and told them he needed them both to stay. By finding a way to make them all work together, Lincoln gained a new sense of control. Always the student, he learned that he needed to include his whole Cabinet on a more regular basis.

In March 1863, a Union draft was announced. This served two purposes. Union forces needed to be reinforced, and the soldiers already in the field needed a morale boost. The term of service for drafted men between the ages of 18 and 45 was three years, which could be avoided by paying $300. Many angry citizens agreed with Congressman Thaddeus Stevens, who said it was "a rich man's bill." The names of the first draftees were listed in July. It was to be a big month for the Union.

In June 1863, Lee invaded the North again and headed for Gettysburg, Pennsylvania. Still searching for the right general, Lincoln had replaced Hooker with George Gordon Meade and sent him to Gettysburg. On July 1 and 2, the two sides battled it out. But on July 3, as the fighting escalated, the Army of the Potomac beat the Confederates back. Meade had stopped Lee from invading the North and crippled his army in the process. Gettysburg was a major victory. However, Meade let Lee's army retreat. Lincoln was beside himself, feeling that the war could have been ended at Gettysburg. "We had them within our grasp. We had only to stretch forth our hands & they were ours." The losses on both sides were staggering. It was the bloodiest battle of the war. The deaths of all American soldiers—Union and Confederate—weighed heavily on Lincoln.

General Ulysses S. Grant's victory at Vicksburg allowed the Union to gain control of the Mississippi River.

Lincoln spent much of his time walking back and forth to the telegraph office in the War Department, to hear news from the battlefields as soon as it came in. Word of another victory in July helped ease his troubles. A few months earlier, in April 1863, Union General Ulysses S. Grant and his men had moved to take the city of Vicksburg, Mississippi. Vicksburg sat on a hill above the Mississippi River and was an important stronghold of the South. By May, Grant was almost there, and winning battles along the way. When he arrived, and could not take the city by force right away, Grant settled in for a siege. On July 4, Vicksburg surrendered to Grant. The American flag flew from the Vicksburg courthouse. The tide was turning, and Lincoln's popularity was on the rise again.

Frederick Douglass had suggested the idea of forming black regiments back in August 1861. He said, "Why does the Government reject the negro? Is he not a man? Can he not wield a sword, fire a gun, march and countermarch, and obey orders like any other?" A year and a half later, the signing of the Emancipation Proclamation encouraged blacks to fight for the Union.

People turn out to celebrate Independence Day as the Stars and Stripes fly over the Vicksburg courthouse on July 4, 1863.

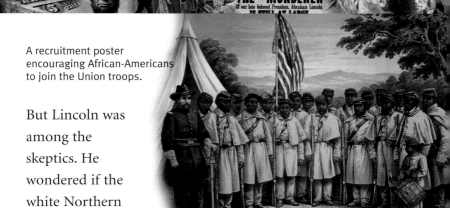

A recruitment poster encouraging African-Americans to join the Union troops.

But Lincoln was among the skeptics. He wondered if the white Northern soldiers would welcome black soldiers. Still, black units began to be organized. Former slaves and Northern free blacks alike took up arms to fight against slavery.

By the spring of 1863, Lincoln was all in favor of recruitment. "The bare sight of fifty thousand armed, and drilled black soldiers on the banks of the Mississippi would end the rebellion at once," he said. The War Department set up the United States Colored Troops in May. These all-black units were led by white officers. By summer, black troops saw action and proved the skeptics wrong. In May, at Port Hudson in Louisiana, they fought. In June, at Milliken's Bend in Louisiana, they fought. In July at Fort Wagner, South Carolina, a regiment of mainly free Northern blacks also fought bravely for their country. By the end of the war, the Union had enlisted more than 180,000 black soldiers. Assistant Secretary of War Charles Dana later wrote, "The bravery of the blacks…completely revolutionized the sentiment of the army with regard to the employment of Negro troops."

Douglass was pleased but pressed for more. He visited the White House in August 1863 asking the president to pay black soldiers the same as white; to give them equality in the Union forces. Lincoln assured him that would come in time. Douglass later said that Lincoln, "in no single instance reminded me…of the difference of color."

On November 18, 1863, Lincoln traveled to Gettysburg to help dedicate a national military cemetery. In the room where he was staying, Lincoln the father and husband worried about his frantic wife and his son Tad, who was home with a fever. Lincoln the president worked at a desk, finishing his thoughts about freedom and democracy and setting them to paper.

The following day, nearly 20,000 people gathered for the dedication. The wasted battlefield, now lined with coffins, was in sight of the platform where Lincoln sat. Another speaker, Edward Everett, former senator and Secretary of State, went before him and spoke for almost two hours. Then it was Lincoln's turn. The towering Lincoln stood and spoke just 272 words, delivering one of the most powerful speeches in American history.

"Four score and seven years ago our fathers brought forth on this continent, a new nation, conceived in Liberty, and dedicated to the proposition that all men are created equal.

"Now we are engaged in a great civil war, testing whether that nation, or any nation so conceived and so dedicated, can long endure. We're met on a great battlefield of that war. We have come to dedicate a portion of that field, as a final

resting place for those who here gave their lives that that nation might live. It is altogether fitting and proper that we should do this.

"But, in a larger sense, we can not dedicate—we can not consecrate—we can not hallow—this ground. The brave men, living and dead, who struggled here, have consecrated it, far above our poor power to add or detract. The world will little note, nor long remember what we say here, but it can never forget what they did here.

It is for us the living, rather, to be dedicated here to the unfinished work which they who fought here have thus far so nobly advanced. It is rather for us to be here dedicated to the great task remaining before us—that from these honored dead we take increased devotion to that cause for which they gave the last full measure of devotion—that we here highly resolve that these dead shall not have died in vain—that this nation, under God, shall have a new birth of freedom—and that

Lincoln's Gettysburg Address was so brief that he finished delivering it before some spectators realized it had started.

government of the people, by the people, for the people, shall not perish from the earth."

11

No Turning Back

Lincoln had not been feeling well. When he returned home from Gettysburg, it was discovered that he had a mild case of smallpox. He had a fever and was contagious. Lincoln was sick for three weeks and confined to his quarters. But his sense of humor shone through. "Now I have something I can give everybody," he said.

While recuperating, Lincoln worked on his plan for reconstructing the nation after war, and asked for input from his Cabinet. It seemed certain that a Union victory was coming, and the president needed to lay out a proposal for bringing the two halves of the troubled nation together again. Lincoln knew he needed a plan that would please as many people as possible. With a rift this big, it was not going to be easy. Republicans and Democrats had vastly different opinions of what should be done. Lincoln carefully crafted a plan that would ease the nation into repair. He needed Southerners to show that they would be loyal to the Union. And Northerners needed to feel satisfied enough by this to welcome them back.

RECONSTRUCTION

Reconstruction was the plan for allowing Confederate states to return to the Union.

To this end, his Proclamation of Amnesty and Reconstruction of December 8, 1863, stated that rebels would have to take

an oath to "faithfully support, protect and defend the Constitution…and the union" and could resume "rights of property, except as to slaves…" High-ranking Confederates were not eligible to take the oath.

Although the plan was well balanced and admired by many, there were those who complained. Some wanted the president to drop the issue of emancipation in exchange for peace with the Confederacy. To that, Lincoln said he was willing to discuss peace, but only if the Confederacy would give up on the issue of slavery— something he knew would

Ulysses S. Grant

Ulysses S. Grant became a symbol of Union victory in the Civil War. When he first volunteered for service in the Civil War, he said, "There are but two parties now, traitors and patriots, and I want hereafter to be ranked with the latter." Later, in 1869, the war hero was elected eighteenth president of the United States.

not happen. Others felt the president had been too lenient on the rebels and had hoped for a more radical reconstruction plan to make them pay for their disloyalty. But Lincoln was more interested in concentrating on the future than worrying about the past. He wanted the war to be over.

Although military progress was slow in the winter of 1863–1864, Grant had shown that he was capable of making great strides for the Union. Lincoln had faith in him and wanted Grant's brand of energy and success to affect all the Union troops. In March 1864, Lincoln promoted him to lieutenant general, in charge of all Union armies. A festive celebration marked the occasion. It was a post that had not been held since George Washington.

Grant soon developed a plan to cripple the South, combining the efforts of several Union armies. As Grant began to lead the effort, he sent news to Lincoln that "there will be no turning back." The losses were devastating—more than 30,000 men dead. Lincoln was horrified. He remembered his childhood days of hating even to see an animal killed. "Could we have avoided this terrible, bloody war!...Is it ever to end!" But Grant did not give up. And Lincoln's faith in him did not fail.

In June, the president took Tad with him to visit Grant and the troops. The visit boosted everyone's morale, including Lincoln's. Throughout the summer, Grant adjusted his strategy to the best of his ability. But there was no easy way. The number of dead climbed.

In August, Lincoln sent word to Grant, who was holding a siege in Petersburg, Virginia, "Hold on with a bull-dog gripe [sic], and chew and choke, as much as possible."

In the month before promoting Grant, Lincoln had called for more recruits. The armies needed an infusion of men.

Grant's siege on Petersburg resulted in the city falling to the Union on April 2, 1865. As the Confederate flag came down, the Union flag was raised.

In February, the call was for 500,000 men. In March, he asked for 200,000 more. People longed for the war to end, and the president's popularity suffered. The radicals were unhappy with his slavery and reconstruction policies, believing they were not sweeping or dramatic enough. The conservatives doubted his leadership abilities. As the summer of 1864 dragged on without victory, many blamed Lincoln. Some urged Grant to run for president, but the general did not yet have any desire to hold that position.

Still enough Republicans got behind Lincoln to secure his renomination in June. Lincoln would run for a second term as president in the 1864 elections. Andrew Johnson was put forth as his running mate for vice president. Lincoln wanted very much to be reelected, "to finish this job of putting down the rebellion, and restoring peace and prosperity to the country."

Lincoln reviews Union troops in 1862. The soldiers were loyal to their president, and he secured the military vote in the 1864 election.

The Democrats nominated George B. McClellan as their presidential candidate—the general who Lincoln had disagreed with on many occasions. McClellan made claims of ending the war with compromise. Learning this, the Confederates rooted for his success.

As the November election approached, Lincoln spent what time he could afford to help his campaign. He asked generals to assist soldiers in getting to the voting stations, if they could not vote from the field. And in October, he admitted Nevada into the Union as its thirty-sixth state. Lincoln sat by the telegraph office in the War Department as the election results started to come in on November 8, 1864.

The election results showed that, although many politicians thought Lincoln was weak and ineffective, the people of the nation loved him. He won by a wide margin, and soldiers were among his strongest supporters. McClellan had been a popular general among his men, but Lincoln

Andrew Johnson

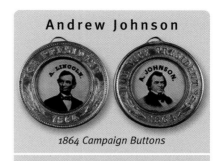

1864 Campaign Buttons

Andrew Johnson had the distinction of being the only southern senator who did not join the Confederacy when his state, Tennessee, seceded from the Union. It made him a very good choice for vice president, because it helped win Democratic votes for Lincoln. Johnson only served six weeks as vice president before having to assume the presidency.

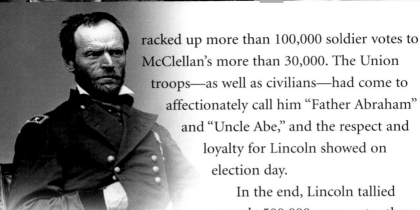

racked up more than 100,000 soldier votes to McClellan's more than 30,000. The Union troops—as well as civilians—had come to affectionately call him "Father Abraham" and "Uncle Abe," and the respect and loyalty for Lincoln showed on election day.

In the end, Lincoln tallied nearly 500,000 more votes than McClellan. Lincoln was thrilled that about four million Americans took the election seriously and voted during a time of such turmoil.

Before securing victory in Atlanta, General William Sherman evacuated the civilians from that city.

Still, the president had enemies. Threats on Lincoln's life were nothing new. Plenty of letters had arrived at the White House hinting at plans to kill or kidnap the president. There were people who were furious that Lincoln was reelected. The election results were enough to put Ward Hill Lamon, Lincoln's long-standing friend and bodyguard, on extra alert. After Lincoln went to bed on the night of November 8,

Lamon gathered knives, pistols, and blankets and camped on the floor right outside Lincoln's bedroom door. He slept there all night, protecting the president.

Certainly the Battle of Atlanta, won by General William Tecumseh Sherman, one of Grant's most trusted leaders, had helped the election victory. Sherman and his men had engaged in a fearsome fight for that city that began in July. On September 1, the rebels fled Atlanta. On September 4, Sherman telegraphed, "Atlanta is ours, and fairly won." It was a badly needed victory.

Lincoln was a beloved president. Items that belonged to him, such as this monogrammed pocket watch and chain, are sought after by collectors and museums.

A few days after the election, Secretary of State Seward, who had long felt superior to Lincoln but had come to admire him greatly, said, "Henceforth all men will come to see him as...I have seen him—a true, loyal, patient, patriotic, and benevolent man."

Union troops ripped up railroads to dismantle the South's transportation system.

95

chapter 12

The End of Slavery

After Sherman's victory in Georgia, the news from the battlefront continued to be good for the Union. In September and October, General Philip H. Sheridan drove the Confederates out of the Shenandoah Valley and destroyed farmlands, cutting off a large food supply for the rebels. And Sherman led some 60,000 men in a march across Georgia. They destroyed more Confederate supplies, farms, buildings, and railroads as they went. The city of Savannah fell to the Union on December 22. A week earlier, General George H. Thomas defeated Confederate General John Bell Hood's large rebel army in Tennessee. The Sherman and Thomas victories, Lincoln said, "brings those who sat in darkness, to see a great light."

"Light" was something that was very much needed in the Lincoln

Sherman's soldiers systematically crippled the South's capacity to wage war in their "march to the sea."

A Presidency of Firsts

Congressional Medal of Honor: In December 1861, Lincoln approved the first Congressional Medal of Honor for the navy. In February 1862, he signed into law the army medal. Both medals honor heroic military actions. Secretary of War Stanton presented the first medals to a group of six men on March 25, 1863. The only woman to have ever received this honor was Mary Walker, for her work as a doctor in the Civil War. The first African-American to be given the medal was William Carney, for his service during the Civil War.

Income tax: During the Civil War, in order to help pay for the huge wartime expenses, Lincoln established the Commissioner of Internal Revenue and created the first income tax—a tax on money earned by individuals—beginning in 1862.

Paper money: The federal government first issued paper money on March 10, 1862. These legal tender notes, also called "greenbacks," were issued in amounts from $1 to $1,000.

The first national banking system was also established.

Free mail delivery: The Post Office Department began delivering mail free of charge to 49 of the nation's largest cities in 1863.

Transcontinental message: The first transcontinental telegraph system, invented by Samuel Morse, was completed on October 24, 1861. Prior to this, the fastest way to send messages long distance was on horseback via the Pony Express.

In God We Trust: On April 22, 1864, Congress passed an act to put "In God We Trust" on federal coins. The words first appeared on the 1864 two-cent coin. Today, those words are on all U.S. coins.

Lincoln cent: Lincoln was the first president to be featured on a U.S. coin. In 1909, Lincoln's profile, from a photo taken of him by Mathew Brady in 1864, was put on the penny. The issue of the Lincoln cent marked the one-hundredth anniversary of his birth.

Lincoln Cent

White House. The war was taking its toll on the president, as well as his family. He told a friend, "This war is eating my life out. I have a strong impression that I shall not live to see the end."

Lincoln looked to the Bible frequently. And as was his pattern in life, Lincoln tried to ease his own stress and fatigue with entertainment. He took trips to the opera and theater with Mary, Tad, and others when he could, and visited with friends.

Mary did her best to support her husband while coping with her own losses.

Mary had been trying to function bravely in the face of everything the nation was suffering, as well as what her family had been through. She visited the wounded and dying soldiers who filled the Washington hospitals in an effort to ease her pain as well as theirs. She took flowers with her to offer a little brightness. But Mary had really not recovered from Willie's death. She had visions of Willie's ghost visiting her and told her sister, "He comes to me every night, and stands at the foot of my bed with the same sweet, adorable smile he always had; he does not always come alone; little Eddie is sometimes with him...." Mary even went to séances in a desperate attempt to contact her dead sons. On at least one occasion,

Lincoln even attended. Mainly he worried for his wife's mental health and felt she was being taken advantage of by the people she hired to run the séances. Heaped on top of the grief she felt about her children, Mary was deathly afraid of someone killing her husband. This fear was not helped by a dream Lincoln told her about, in which he had been assassinated.

When their oldest son Robert wanted to take leave from Harvard and join the service, Mary was beside herself. She had already lost two children. She could not bear the thought of losing Robert, too. The Lincolns disagreed about it. Mary said, "I am so frightened he may never come back to us." To which Lincoln replied, "Many a poor mother, Mary, has had to make this sacrifice…" In the end, Robert did join General Grant's staff in February 1865.

To satisfy both his and his wife's concerns, Lincoln had his son Robert placed in a relatively safe position on Grant's staff.

After Lincoln was once again elected president in November 1864, his attention turned toward encouraging a constitutional amendment to outlaw slavery. He believed his attitude toward slavery had a lot to do with winning the election. The time was right for pushing the issue further. The Emancipation Proclamation

A postage stamp commemorates the passing of the 13th Amendment.

had been an important first step, but it had only made slavery illegal in the rebel states. And it was only a temporary measure, because it could be overturned if challenged. But the Thirteenth Amendment to the Constitution, which Congress had been considering, would make slavery illegal anywhere in the United States—*permanently*. Lincoln wanted it passed as soon as possible.

On January 31, 1865, Congress voted. The Thirteenth Amendment passed 119 to 56. Can you imagine how momentous an occasion this was? Republicans—and even some Democrats—cheered and hugged and hollered. Some even cried tears of joy and relief. Spectators in the gallery joined in the celebration, including blacks who were welcomed inside for the first time in history. On Capitol Hill, cannon were fired in celebration. One Congressman wrote, "I have felt, ever since the vote, as if I were in a new country." Although it had taken the right circumstances and the right timing to achieve this "moral victory," as Lincoln called it, the Thirteenth Amendment reflected his long-held belief that "if slavery is not wrong, nothing is wrong." Frederick Douglass, who had continually urged the president to take a stronger stance on slavery, was delighted.

A few days after the amendment was passed, an attempt to discuss peace was made aboard the president's steamboat, the *River Queen*. Nothing came of it, as Lincoln was unwilling to accept any terms that did not include the seceded states returning to the Union. The February 3, 1865, peace talks failed. Peace would come only with a military victory.

The peace talks aboard the *River Queen* did not succeed. When George P. A. Healy painted this in 1868, he added the rainbow as a symbol of peace.

chapter 13

With Malice Toward None

The following month, Lincoln was inaugurated for the second time. March 4, 1865, was a rainy, windy day. The unpaved streets were thick with mud. Washington was teeming with visitors who had traveled to witness the occasion. By noon, the huge crowd awaiting the president's swearing in was likely chilled and soaked. Vice President Andrew Johnson took his oath inside the Senate. Having had too much to drink to settle his nerves, his speech rambled on, at times incoherently. Lincoln asked that Johnson not speak once the

A crowd gathers to hear Lincoln's second inaugural speech.

Abraham Lincoln

Lincoln's March 4, 1865, speech included his famous words "With malice toward none..."

the sword, as was said ... thousand years ago, so still it must be said "the judgments of the Lord, are true and righteous altogether."
With malice toward none; with charity for all; with firmness in the right, as God gives us to see the right, let us strive on to finish the work we are in; to bind up the nation's wounds; to care for him who shall have borne the battle, and for his widow, and his orphan— to do all which may achieve and cherish a just and a lasting peace, among ourselves, and with all nations.

ceremony continued outside in public.

When Lincoln stepped out onto the inaugural platform constructed in front of the Capitol Building, the crowd began to cheer. As if on cue, the sun poked through the clouds just as Lincoln began to speak.

Lincoln's second inaugural speech was intentionally short. He did not believe it was the time to speak of Union victories. Instead, he wanted to relay his thoughts on what the war was all about, and what it meant to the nation. He was careful in his choice of words not to point blame. He did not refer to North or South. Lincoln said, "All dreaded it—all sought to avert it.…but one of them would make war rather than let the nation survive; and the other would accept war rather than let it perish. And the war came.…" He continued, "Fondly do we hope—fervently do we pray—that this mighty scourge of war may speedily pass away.…With malice toward none; with charity for all; with firmness in the right, as God gives us to see the right, let us strive on to finish the work we are in; to bind up the nation's wounds; to care for him who shall have borne the battle, and for his widow, and his orphan—to

103

do all which may achieve and cherish a just, and a lasting peace, among ourselves, and with all nations."

The speech was met with thunderous clapping and cheering. That night, at the inaugural reception at the White House, police tried to keep Frederick Douglass from entering. But Lincoln sent word to let him in—the first time an African-American had ever attended an inaugural reception. The president was delighted when Douglass told him he thought the speech a "sacred effort."

Far from the inexperienced man who first took office, Lincoln was now a seasoned leader. During his presidency, Lincoln assumed more powers than any previous president. And he did so with great respect for the office and the nation, exercising his power with caution during a perilous time in history. When he felt it necessary to take emergency measures during a wartime crisis, such as suspending the writ of habeas corpus or suppressing hostile newspapers, he did. Harriet Beecher Stowe said of him, "Lincoln certainly was the safest leader a nation could have…A reckless, bold, theorizing, dashing man of genius might have wrecked our Constitution and ended us in a splendid military despotism."

Meanwhile, the nation's crisis was still taking its toll on the Lincoln marriage. Abraham and Mary had long had a turbulent relationship. Given the circumstances, and their personalities, that seems hardly a surprise. Lincoln was not particularly affectionate, he was moody, had not been feeling well, and was often lost in thought when they were together.

Mary still suffered from the loss of her two children. She frequently worried that her husband was in danger. And she had a secret plaguing her. Mary was terrified that Lincoln would discover her extravagant spending, as shopping had become her way of coping with stress. She had overspent her budget by many thousands.

But most importantly, the two now differed in their feelings about the war. Lincoln's love for the Union made him deeply committed to rejoining North and South without interest in revenge for the bloody past. Mary, however, saw it much differently. She *did* want the South to pay. The war had torn her family apart—she had lost brothers to the Confederacy who then ultimately died in battle, and a distance had grown between Mary and her husband. Despite their troubles, letters and exchanges between husband and wife show that they continued to love each other. While apart, Lincoln wrote to Mary, "I really wish to see you."

The scene of Lincoln's second inaugural ball. Mary is dressed in pink and white.

chapter 14

Beginning of the End

On March 23, Lincoln set off to visit General Grant and his troops at Grant's headquarters at City Point, Virginia. The trip also gave Lincoln a chance to visit with his son Robert. Mary and Tad went with him, aboard the *River Queen*. Young Tad had a grand old time, exploring the ship and tagging along after his father. Lincoln visited thousands of wounded soldiers—both Union and Confederate—in a field hospital, making a point of shaking every single hand. Lincoln also saw some of the troops in action. He did not have much time to spend with Mary. Already on edge, her temper was about to burst.

As his father grappled with the seriousness of the war, young Tad experienced the excitement. Here he is dressed as a soldier.

One day, Lincoln rode out on horseback with the other men to see General Edward Ord's troops. Mary and Grant's wife, Julia, traveled in an ambulance a bit behind them. When their carriage got to the site, the visit had already begun. And instead of Mary by Lincoln's side, Ord's wife was there. Mary was furious. She accused the woman of flirting with her husband in a public display that embarrassed the president and made Ord's wife cry! Both Lincoln and Julia Grant tried to calm Mary down, but she was beside herself, unable to contain her stress any longer. At dinner that night, she yelled some more. Mary then spent the next few days in her cabin on the *River Queen*. On April 1, she returned to Washington. Tad remained with his father. As soon as Mary got home, she telegraphed her husband to let him know she missed him and that she wanted to return to his side.

The president had been in poor health for some time. He had even held a Cabinet meeting in his room, while he lay sick in bed. But the trip to City Point made him feel much better. And on April 1, the news from Grant must have made him feel positively great. That day, Grant sent Confederate flags that had been captured on the battlefield in Petersburg to the *River Queen* as a gift for Lincoln. The president said, "Here is something material, something I can see, feel, and understand. This means victory. This *is* victory." In fact, victory was near.

On March 27, Lincoln had met with Grant and Sherman on the *River Queen* to discuss how to handle a Confederate surrender. Lincoln still felt no need to punish the rebels; he wanted the nation rejoined. He wanted Confederate soldiers to be able to return home, to their families and jobs. He did indicate that he hoped the high-ranking officials, especially Jefferson Davis, would slink away, never to bother anyone again. He said, "If they stay, they will be punished for their crimes."

Confederate General Lee knew that a defeat at Petersburg meant Richmond was next. He sent word to Jefferson Davis, whose home and headquarters were in that Confederate capital, to have the city evacuated. Word quickly spread throughout Richmond, and hordes of people fled the city. As the Confederate soldiers left, they set fire to bridges and supplies to slow the Union Army. Fire swept through the city. By April 3, Richmond was in ruins.

The following day, Lincoln went to Richmond to see the city for himself. The black people there greeted him joyously, calling out to shake his hand and crowding around the man who

Richmond, Virginia, suffered extensive damage in the war. Deliberately set fires were whipped up by wind and tore through town uncontrollably.

had put an end to slavery. "Glory!" said one woman. "God bless you," said another. One man even kneeled before the president, but Lincoln said to him, "Don't kneel to me. That is not right. You must kneel to God only; and thank him for the liberty you will enjoy hereafter."

Jefferson Davis's home had been turned into Union military headquarters, and Lincoln headed there to rest. When he sat down in Davis's chair, Union soldiers whooped and hollered. Meanwhile, Lee and his Confederate troops fled west, pursued by Union troops.

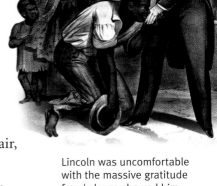

Lincoln was uncomfortable with the massive gratitude freed slaves showed him for his actions.

By April 7, Union troops led by Sheridan had blocked Lee's retreat near Appomattox, Virginia. Grant sent word to Lee, asking for his surrender. Lee wanted to know the terms. Grant wired back on April 8, "There is but one condition I would insist upon, namely; that the men and officers surrendered shall be disqualified for taking up arms again, against the Government of the United States."

Mary, having composed herself, had returned to City Point on April 6, to meet her husband, who was back from touring Richmond. A few days later, they all ferried back to

Ulysses S. Grant

Robert E. Lee

Near Appomattox, Virginia, General Lee's troops were cornered. He realized the end was at hand and surrendered to Grant.

Washington. On the evening of April 9, Secretary of War Stanton delivered the victorious telegram. Lee had surrendered to Grant at the Appomattox Court House. The war was all but over.

Bands played, flags flew, fireworks burst in the sky, people sang and cried and cheered outside the White House and in the streets of Washington. Tad waved a Confederate flag from a White House window. On April 11, Lincoln gave a speech to the crowds that celebrated on the White House grounds. He spoke from a second-story window. Amid the jubilation, though, Lincoln kept a cool head. He was not interested in gloating or cheering about the victory, as perhaps many in the crowd would have wanted. Instead, he wanted to caution people to think carefully about how the Union would be rebuilt—reconstructed—peacefully, how North and South could come back together again, and be one friendly nation. He knew people disagreed about how to proceed and talked about how difficult it would be to rebuild the nation. Lincoln also put forth the idea of giving African-Americans the right to vote. This suggestion was certainly a presidential first.

By the end of May, the last army of Confederate troops would surrender. But Lincoln would not live to see it. His views were still unpopular with many, including people in the North who felt he had taken too many liberties. Lincoln had continued to receive many pieces of hate mail and death threats. One man who hated him would prove deadly. John Wilkes Booth, listening to the president speak about voting rights for blacks, vowed to rid the world of Lincoln. "That is the last speech he will ever make," he said.

The mentally unstable John Wilkes Booth set his sights on Lincoln.

chapter 15

A Giant Falls

On April 14, Lincoln woke up feeling better than he had in months. The relief of the war coming to an end was written all over his face. In fact, four days earlier, he had had his picture taken, and the image captured a look of calm and happiness that had not shown much on the president's face for four years.

On the morning of the fourteenth, there was more cause for family celebration. Robert returned home from war and joined his parents for breakfast. Robert shared a rare long talk with his father, filling him in on the details of the surrender. Since Robert was one of Grant's officers, he had been at Appomattox Court House for the historic event. They also discussed Robert's return to Harvard and the boy's future.

After breakfast, the weary Robert went upstairs for a nap while Lincoln, Mary, and Tad went on an

This is the last photograph of Lincoln, taken just four days before he died.

outing. There was also a Cabinet meeting that morning. One Cabinet member said, "I never saw Mr. Lincoln so cheerful and happy." Afterward, he enjoyed an apple as he attended to more work in his office. Then the president met with visitors before he and Mary set off on a carriage ride together—a date they had made two days earlier. In this time of relaxation, the two seemed to be making heartfelt strides toward smoothing over their recent rocky past.

The accounts of their carriage ride leave the impression of a couple who loved each other, had shared a lot in life, and looked forward to carrying on together. Mary commented on how happy he seemed. He talked about the war being over and the hardships they had endured and how they were ready for an easier time. Lincoln said, "We must both be more cheerful in the future; between the war and the loss of our darling Willie, we have both been very miserable." He talked about making plans to travel together for a while and then return to Springfield and settle down again. After their ride, Lincoln and Mary went back to the White House for dinner. Mary had developed a headache, but Lincoln said they must keep their plans to attend the theater that evening because it had been advertised in the newspaper and people were expecting to see him there. He was also looking forward to it, as he always welcomed the fun of going to the theater.

When Lincoln and Mary arrived at Ford's Theatre at 8:30, the play, *Our American Cousin*, was already in progress. But the moment Lincoln appeared, everything stopped and the orchestra struck up "Hail to the Chief" in honor of the president. The audience stood and cheered. Then Mary, Lincoln, and their guests, Major Henry Rathbone and Clara Harris, took their seats in the presidential box. Lincoln sat in a rocking chair put in the box especially for him. As the comedy on stage continued, Mary clapped and Lincoln laughed. They seemed to be enjoying themselves. Mary was snuggled up against Lincoln, holding his hand. She wondered aloud to her husband, "What will Miss Harris think of my hanging on to you so?" Lincoln replied, "She won't think anything about it." They were the last words he spoke.

A series of events were about to unfold that had been in the planning stages since Lincoln's April 11 speech. Actor and Confederate sympathizer John Wilkes Booth had engineered an elaborate assassination plot, complete with accomplices. It was not Booth's first attempt to harm the president. He had mapped out several kidnapping plans that had fallen

Ford's Theatre on April 14, 1865. The decorated presidential box is shown at right.

through when Lincoln's schedule changed. These failures made Booth even more determined to carry through with his final plot against the president. And on April 14, when he read in the paper that Lincoln would be at Ford's Theatre that very night, Booth went into action. There is some evidence that Booth's actions were either known about, or approved by, the Confederate Secret Service.

The rocking chair Lincoln was sitting in when he was shot.

Since Booth was a well-known actor with connections to the theater, he had no problem walking right upstairs toward the entrance to the presidential box a little after 10:00 PM. The policeman who was on guard in the hallway had left his post. Standing outside the box was a White House guard named Charles Forbes. Booth showed Forbes identification and was allowed in. Once inside, Booth barred the door. He crept up right behind Lincoln, drew out his derringer gun, and fired at the president's head from close range. It was 10:13.

Lincoln slumped forward. Mary screamed. Major Rathbone went for Booth, but Booth pulled out a dagger and slashed Rathbone's arm. Then Booth leaped over the edge of the box, down onto the stage. He broke his leg in the process, but still

115

John Wilkes Booth

John Wilkes Booth was an actor who thrived on drama in all parts of his life. Even offstage, and from childhood, Booth was known for spinning wild tales. His hatred of Lincoln and his loyalty to the Confederacy fed his visions of avenging the South.

managed to escape out the back of the theater amid all the cries and confusion.

The attack on the president was not the only one that night. Booth's plan also included assaults by two of his accomplices. George Atzerodt was instructed to kill Vice President Andrew Johnson. And Lewis Paine was sent to kill Secretary of State William Seward. Atzerodt could not bring himself to follow Booth's orders. But Paine was a different story.

At the same time that Booth shot Lincoln, Paine stormed into the Seward home on a rampage. Seward was in bed at the time, recuperating from a broken jaw he had gotten in a carriage accident. When Seward's adult son Frederick blocked Paine's way, and Paine's gun wouldn't fire, he cracked Frederick over the head with it. Paine then pushed his way into William Seward's room. Encountering Seward's daughter, he knocked her unconscious and then began stabbing Seward in the neck. After horribly wounding Seward, Paine flew back down the stairs and out the door,

slashing his knife into anybody who stood in his way. Several people were badly wounded. In the end, Seward's life was saved by the metal brace around his neck.

Meanwhile, in the aftermath of the shooting at Ford's Theatre, Lincoln was quickly being moved to William Petersen's boardinghouse across the street. Several doctors who had been in the audience had rushed to Lincoln's side. The bullet had entered behind his left ear and was lodged behind his right eye. The situation was grim. The men carried Lincoln's still form to a bedroom in the boardinghouse. The president's body was too long for the bed, so he was laid diagonally in it, with his feet sticking over the end. For the next nine hours, doctors did what they could. Mary sat beside him, crying and begging him to speak to her. Robert came, too, and wept. People gathered in the street outside, in the rain, united in a vigil for the president. At 7:22 AM, on April 15, 1865, Lincoln took his last breath.

Rewards were offered for any information leading to the killer and his accomplices.

Lincoln was the first president in American

history to have been assassinated. Like the crowd outside the boardinghouse, much of the nation united in their grief over the president's death. Even many who disagreed with his politics and had angrily criticized him mourned. Flags were lowered to half-mast. Black cloth draped buildings. And people all over America wore badges of mourning pinned to their clothes.

The president's body was taken to the White House. Mary shut herself in a guest room, hysterical, and unable to talk to anyone but Tad. On Tuesday, the president's body was on view for the public to pay their respects. People waited in a line that stretched for a mile. A "Temple of Death" had been constructed in the East Room of the White House. The mirrors and chandeliers were draped in black. Lincoln lay in a coffin on a platform decorated with black satin and velvet in the center of the room. Thousands of people

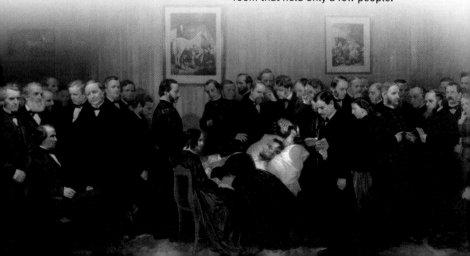

Although this painting shows many mourners by the president's bedside, Lincoln spent his last hours in a tiny room that held only a few people.

streamed through in an
orderly fashion, stopping
at the coffin to grieve for
the president. The following
morning, Lincoln's funeral
was held in the East Room.
Mary, still upstairs in
bed, could not bring herself
to attend.

The tall president's legs hung
off the side of this bed, in
which he died.

People had been streaming
into Washington in order to pay their last respects to the
president. Hotels were overflowing, and people with blankets
slept on the grass in the parks. Inside the East Room, Grant
stood near the president's head, in tears. Robert stood at the
foot. Other officials were all around. After the service, a
funeral procession slowly carried Lincoln's coffin to the
Capitol Building. Soldiers and citizens marched behind,
including some 4,000 black citizens paying tribute to their
fallen president. On Thursday, more of the public came to
mourn as he lay in state at the Capitol.

On Friday morning, April 21, Lincoln's body was again
moved. This time, it was to embark on the reverse presidential
train ride that had brought him to Washington four years
earlier. Lincoln was on his way home to Illinois. Willie, who
had died three years earlier, was moved with his father.
Willie's body was carefully removed from a Washington
cemetery and placed aboard the train.

The funeral procession in Washington, D.C. As his body was moved to Illinois, 11 more funerals were held before Lincoln was buried.

Eleven more ceremonies for Lincoln were held in cities between Washington and Springfield. In New York City alone, more than 85,000 people came out. On May 3, the procession arrived at the Illinois State House. The next morning it was on to the Oak Ridge Cemetery in Springfield, where Willie and Lincoln were laid to rest.

Several days earlier, while much of the country focused on saying good-bye, police were still hot on the trail of the assassin. On April 26, John Wilkes Booth was cornered in his hiding spot inside a tobacco barn not 60 miles from Washington. Booth was killed in the struggle to capture him. Eight of his suspected accomplices were also captured, and four were hanged for their crimes.

Lincoln was dead, slavery was abolished, and the war was over. Still, Jefferson Davis clung to his last hopes. He tried to flee westward but was captured in Georgia on May 10. Meanwhile, a smattering of fighting still went on in pockets of the West, and in Mississippi, Louisiana, and Alabama. The last recorded death of the Civil War occurred during a

Confederate victory in Texas on May 13, 1865. Many other soldiers were still making their way back home.

Although slavery was officially ended, there was no "happily ever after" ending to the story that dominated Lincoln's presidency. The loss of life was staggering. More than 600,000 died as a result of the war, and more than 300,000 were wounded. The economy of the South was in a shambles. And Reconstruction was a slow and complicated process, which did not fulfill Lincoln's vision. In the South, whites were not ready to welcome black people into their society. Blacks had freedom, but equal rights were a long way off.

Even so, without Abraham Lincoln, progress would have been dramatically slowed. There is no question that Lincoln made great strides for the nation. It may even be said that he did more for the antislavery cause than any other single human being. The ideals that he pursued for the nation, that all Americans should have the chance to create a good and happy life, are the ideals that America still strives for today.

One of Lincoln's most praiseworthy characteristics was his ability to continue to grow and learn as he guided the nation. All people have flaws, but this quality made him a great president able to lead during a very difficult time. Secretary of War Stanton recognized this greatness and said, as he stood by Lincoln's deathbed, "Now he belongs to the ages."

Events in the Life of Abraham Lincoln

February 12, 1809
Abraham Lincoln is born in Hardin County, Kentucky.

November 4, 1842
Lincoln marries Mary Todd in Springfield, Illinois.

May 18, 1860
Lincoln wins Republican Party's nomination for president

January 1837
Lincoln votes against proslavery resolutions in Illinois legislature.

August 3, 1846
Lincoln is elected to Congress.

December 2, 1819
Thomas Lincoln marries Sarah Bush Johnston.

May 1854
The Kansas-Nebraska Act is passed.

October 5, 1818
Nancy Hanks Lincoln dies from milk sickness.

August 4, 1834
Lincoln is elected to the Illinois state legislature.

CHARLESTON

MERCURY

EXTRA:

THE

UNION

IS

DISSOLVED!

March 1, 1837
Lincoln is officially licensed to practice law.

June 16, 1858
Lincoln gives "house divided" speech in accepting the Republican Party's nomination to run for Senate

December 1860
South Carolina becomes the first state to secede from the Union.

April 12, 1861
The first shots of the Civil War are fired at Fort Sumter.

April 14, 1865
John Wilkes Booth shoots Lincoln at Ford's Theatre. The president dies the next morning.

March 4, 1865
Lincoln is inaugurated president for a second term.

January 1, 1863
Lincoln signs the Emancipation Proclamation.

January 31, 1865
The Thirteenth Amendment is passed abolishing slavery.

May 30, 1922
Memorial Day dedication of the Lincoln Memorial in Washington, D.C.

March 4, 1861
Lincoln is inaugurated as the sixteenth president.

November 19, 1863
Lincoln gives the Gettysburg Address.

April 9, 1865
Lee surrenders to Grant at the Appomattox Courthouse.

October 31, 1941
Mount Rushmore is completed.

Bibliography

Books:

Bak, Richard. *The Day Lincoln Was Shot.* Dallas, TX: Taylor Publishing Company, 1998.

Basler, Roy P., ed. *Abraham Lincoln: His Speeches and Writings.* Cambridge, MA: Da Capo Press, 2001.

Burlingame, Michael. *The Inner World of Abraham Lincoln.* Chicago, IL: University of Illinois Press, 1994.

Donald, David Herbert. *Lincoln.* New York: Simon & Schuster, 1995.

_____. *We Are Lincoln Men: Abraham Lincoln and His Friends.* New York: Simon & Schuster, 2003.

Gienapp, William E. *This Fiery Trial: The Speeches and Writings of Abraham Lincoln.* New York: Oxford University Press, 2002.

_____. *Abraham Lincoln and Civil War America.* New York: Oxford University Press, 2002.

Guelzo, Allen C. *Abraham Lincoln: Redeemer President.* Grand Rapids, MI: William B. Eerdmans Publishing, 1999.

_____. *Lincoln's Emancipation Proclamation: The End of Slavery in America.* New York: Simon & Schuster, 2004.

Kunhardt, Dorothy Meserve and Kunhardt, Philip B. Jr. *Twenty Days.* Seacaucus, NJ: Newcastle Publishing, 1985.

Kunhardt, Philip B. Jr., Kunhardt, Philip B. III, and Kunhardt, Peter W. *Lincoln: An Illustrated Biography.* New York: Knopf, 1997.

McPherson, James. *Battle Cry of Freedom: The Civil War Era.* New York: Oxford University Press, 1998.

_____. *Abraham Lincoln and the Second American Revolution.* New York: Oxford University Press, 1991.

Oates, Stephen B. *With Malice Toward None: A Life of Abraham Lincoln.* New York: HarperCollins, 1994.

_____. *Abraham Lincoln: The Man Behind the Myths.* New York: HarperPerennial, 1994.

Pinsker, Matthew. *Lincoln's Sanctuary: Abraham Lincoln and the Soldiers' Home.* New York: Oxford University Press, 2003.

Richardson, Robert Dale, ed. *Abraham Lincoln's Autobiography.* Boston, MA: The Beacon Press, 1948.

Speer, Bonnie Stahlman. *The Great Abraham Lincoln Hijack.* Norman, OK: Reliance Press, 1997.

Sullivan, George. *Picturing Lincoln: Famous Photographs that Popularized the President.* New York: Clarion, 2000.

Tarbell, Ida. *In the Footsteps of the Lincolns.* New York: Harper & Brothers, 1924.

Thomas, Benjamin P. *Abraham Lincoln.* New York: Modern Library, 1968.

Turner, Justin G. and Turner, Linda Levitt. *Mary Todd Lincoln: Her Life and Letters.* New York: Knopf, 1972.

Ward, Geoffrey. *The Civil War: An Illustrated History.* New York: Knopf, 2002.

Winik, Jay. *April 1865.* New York: HarperCollins, 2001.

Films:

Grubin, David. Written by David Grubin and Geoffrey C. Ward. *Abraham and Mary Lincoln: A House Divided.* American Experience, in association with PBS, 2001.

Kunhardt, Peter W. Written by Philip B. Kunhardt III and Philip B. Kunhardt, Jr. *Lincoln.*

Article:

Kunhardt, Dorothy Meserve. "Moving Lincoln's Body." *Life.* February 15, 1963, pp. 398–399.

Sources Cited

Page 15-16: "…he must understand everything…" *With Malice Toward None*, p. 10.

Page 16: "Abraham Lincoln his hand and pen…" *With Malice Toward None*, p. 11.

Page 18-19: "…I could scarcely believe…that I, a poor boy…" *Lincoln: An Illustrated Biography*, p. 43.

Page 30-31: "a drop of honey catches more flies…" and "persuasion, kind unassuming persuasion" *With Malice Toward None*, p. 38.

Page 30-31: "proud fabric of freedom," "jealousy, envy, and avarice," "throw printing presses into rivers," and "reason, cold, calculating, unimpassioned reason," *Abraham Lincoln: His Speeches and Writings*, pp. 80, 83, 84, 85.

Page 32: "…eight or ten choice spirits assembled" and "he did not seek company" *Lincoln: An Illustrated Biography*, p. 52.

Page 33: "he disclosed his whole heart to me," *We Are Lincoln Men: Abraham Lincoln and His Friends*, p. 34.

Page 34: "Mary could make a bishop forget his prayers." *Mary Todd Lincoln: Her Life and Letters*, p. 11.

Page 36: "I am now the most miserable man living." *Abraham Lincoln: His Speeches and Writings*, p. 115.

Page 37: "…hold the question an open one." *We Are Lincoln Men: Abraham Lincoln and His Friends*, p. 43.

Page 38: "When I have a particular case in hand…" *Lincoln*, p. 99.

Page 39: "Persuade our neighbors to compromise…" *Lincoln: An Illustrated Biography*, p. 77.

Page 42: "From 1849 to 1854…" *Abraham Lincoln's Autobiography*, pp. 23-24.

Page 45: "take down the books…" *The Inner World of Abraham Lincoln*, p. 57.

Page 45: "I know every step of the process…" *Lincoln*, p. 159.

Page 46: "When you can't find it anywhere else, look in this." *Abraham Lincoln and Civil War America*, 42.

Page 46: "…no one's laugh was heartier than his." *Abraham Lincoln and Civil War America*, 42.

Page 47: "My childhood's home I see again…" *Lincoln*, 116.

Page 50: "little lady who made this big war." *Lincoln*, 542.

Page 51: "…as he had never been aroused before." *With Malice Toward None*, p.108.

Page 51: "It is wrong, wrong in its…effect," *Lincoln: An Illustrated Biography*, p. 105.

Page 53: "Stranger, do you know where Lincoln lives?" *Lincoln*, p. 197.

Page 54: "assailed, and sneered at, and construed…" *Abraham Lincoln and Civil War America*, pp. 57-58.

Page 54: "A house divided against itself cannot stand," *Abraham Lincoln: His Speeches and Writings*, p. 372.

Page 55: "I shall have my hands full…" *Abraham Lincoln and Civil War America*, p. 61.

Page 56: "I am not, nor ever have been in favor…" *This Fiery Trial: The Speeches and Writings of Abraham Lincoln*, p. 57.

Page 57: "blowing out the moral lights around us." *This Fiery Trial: The Speeches and Writings of Abraham Lincoln*, p. 56.

Page 57: "The real issue in this controversy…" *This Fiery Trial: The Speeches and Writings of Abraham Lincoln*, pp. 64, 66.

Page 57: "I believe I have made some marks…" *Lincoln*, p. 229.

Page 57: "I expect everyone to desert me except Billy." *Lincoln*, p. 228.

Page 58: "Wrong as we think slavery is…" *This Fiery Trial: The Speeches and Writings of Abraham Lincoln*, pp. 80-81.

Page 59: "Just think of such a sucker as me as President." *Lincoln*, p. 235.

Page 59: "The taste is in my mouth a little." *Lincoln*, p. 241.

Page 61: "The evil days…" and "The South should arm at once." *Lincoln: An Illustrated Biography*, p. 133.

Page 65-66: "Before entering upon so grave a matter…" *Abraham Lincoln: His Speeches and Writings*, pp. 64, 66.

Pages 67: "and that, if such attempt be not resisted…" *Lincoln*, p. 292.

Pages 69: "It presents to the whole family of man, the question…" *This Fiery Trial: The Speeches and Writings of Abraham Lincoln*, pp. 99, 105.

Pages 70: "I can do it all." *Lincoln*, p. 319.

Pages 71-72: "It would stink in the land to have it said…" *Abraham Lincoln and Civil War America*, p. 93-94.

Page 73: "My poor boy, he was too good for this earth…" *With Malice Toward None*, p. 290.

Page 74: "Your race are suffering…" *This Fiery Trial: The Speeches and Writings of Abraham Lincoln*, p. 131.

Page 76: "as the last measure of an exhausted government…" *Lincoln*, p. 366.

Page 77: "I expect to maintain this contest until successful…" *Lincoln*, p. 359.

Page 79: "as a fit and necessary war measure…" *Abraham Lincoln: His Speeches and Writings*, pp. 690-691.

Page 80: "Will you pardon me for asking…" *The Inner World of Abraham Lincoln*, p. 186.

Page 81: "My god! My god! What will the country say!" *Lincoln*, p. 436.

Page 83: "We had them within our grasp." *With Malice Toward None*, p. 352.

Page 84: "Why does the Government reject the Negro?" *Lincoln: An Illustrated Biography*, p. 157.

Page 85: "The bare sight of fifty thousand armed…," *Lincoln*, p. 431.

Page 85-86: "The bravery of the blacks…" *Battle Cry of Freedom: The Civil War Era*, p. 634.

Page 86: "in no single instance reminded me…" *With Malice Toward None*, p. 357.

Page 86-87: "Four score and seven years ago…" *Abraham Lincoln: His Speeches and Writings*, p. 734.

Page 88: "Now I have something I can give everybody." *Lincoln*, p. 467.

Page 89: "faithfully support, protect, and defend the Constitution…" *Abraham Lincoln: His Speeches and Writings*, p. 739.

Page 89: "There are but two parties now, traitors and patriots," *The Civil War: An Illustrated History*, p. 49.

Page 90: "there will be no turning back." *Lincoln*, p. 500.

Page 90: "Could we have avoided this terrible, bloody war!" *Lincoln*, p. 500.

Page 91: "Hold on with a bull-dog gripe…" *Abraham Lincoln and Civil War America*, p. 165.

Page 92: "to finish this job of putting down the rebellion…" *Lincoln*, p. 540.

Page 95: "Atlanta is ours, and fairly won." *Lincoln*, p. 530.

Page 95: "Henceforth all men will come to see him as…" *We Are Lincoln Men: Abraham Lincoln and His Friends*, p. 176.

Page 96: "brings those who sat in darkness, to see a great light." *Lincoln*, p. 553.

Page 98: "This war is eating my life out." *With Malice Toward None*, p. 380.

Page 98: "…he comes to me every night," *With Malice Toward None*, p. 376.

Page 99: "I am so frightened…" and "Many a poor mother," *With Malice Toward None*, p. 376.

Page 100: "I have felt, ever since the vote…" *Battle Cry of Freedom: The Civil War Era*, p. 840.

Page 101: "if slavery is not wrong, nothing is wrong." *This Fiery Trial: The Speeches and Writings of Abraham Lincoln*, p. 194.

Page 103-104: "All dreaded it—all sought to avert it…" *This Fiery Trial: The Speeches and Writings of Abraham Lincoln*, p. 220-221.

Page 104: "Lincoln certainly was the safest leader a nation could have…" *Lincoln: An Illustrated Biography*, p. 327.

Page 105: "I really wish to see you." *Lincoln's Sanctuary: Abraham Lincoln and the Soldiers' Home*, p. 122.

Page 107: "Here is something material," *With Malice Toward None*, p. 420.

Page 107: "if they stay, they will be punished for their crimes." *Abraham Lincoln: Redeemer President*, p. 422.

Page 109: "Don't kneel to me." *Battle Cry of Freedom: The Civil War Era*, p. 847.

Page 109: "…there is but one condition I would insist upon," *The Civil War: An Illustrated History*, p. 377.

Page 111: "That is the last speech he will ever make." *Abraham Lincoln and Civil War America*, p. 200.

Page 113: "I never saw Mr. Lincoln so cheerful and happy." *With Malice Toward None*, p. 427.

Page 113: "We must both be more cheerful in the future;" *Lincoln*, p. 593.

Page 114: "What will Miss Harris think…" *Lincoln: An Illustrated Biography*, p. 352.

Page 121: "Now he belongs to the ages." *Lincoln: An Illustrated Biography*, p. 359.

For Further Study

Visit the **Lincoln Memorial** in Washington, D.C. The famous marble sculpture of Lincoln by artist Daniel Chester French sits in the inner room of the memorial entrance. (http://www.nps.gov/linc/)

Visit the **Ford's Theatre National Historic Site** in Washington, D.C. It is simultaneously a working theater and a memorial to Lincoln, with the presidential box restored to look exactly as it did on April 14, 1865. Across the street is Peterson House, where Lincoln died. (http://www.fordstheatre.org/Pages/history/history.htm)

The **Abraham Lincoln Birthplace National Historic Site** is in Hodgenville, Kentucky. A cabin similar to the kind Lincoln grew up in is on display inside the memorial. (http://www.nps.gov/abli/)

The **Lincoln Home National Historic Site** is in Springfield, Illinois. The only house Lincoln owned, where he lived for 17 years, has been restored to look as it did in the 1860s. (http://www.nps.gov/liho/)

Also in Springfield, at the Oak Ridge Cemetery, is the **Lincoln Tomb State Historic Site**. Lincoln is buried there, along with Mary, Eddie, Willie, and Tad. (http://www.state.il.us/hpa/hs/Tomb.htm)

About the Author

Tanya Lee Stone was an editor of children's books for thirteen years before becoming a children's author. Since that time, she has been engaging young readers with her more than seventy-five books on topics that include science, nature, history, and biography. She also writes fiction for young people. Looking back, Stone has always been a writer. She started her first stories at the age of 6. (*Henry the Happy House*, sadly, was never published!) As a student at Oberlin College, she studied English, creative writing, history, and music. Later, she received a Masters in Education degree. Stone now lives in Vermont with her husband and their two wonderful children. She often travels to visit schools and talk about books with young people.
To learn more about Stone and her books, visit *www.tanyastone.com*

Other DK Biographies you may enjoy:

DK Biography: *Anne Frank*
by Kem Knapp Sawyer
ISBN 0-7566-0341-2 paperback
ISBN 0-7566-0490-7 hardcover

DK Biography: *George Washinngton*
by Kem Knapp Sawyer
ISBN 0-7566-0341-2 paperback
ISBN 0-7566-0490-7 hardcover

DK Biography: *Helen Keller*
by Leslie Garrett
ISBN 0-7566-0339-0 paperback
ISBN 0-7566-0488-5 hardcover

DK Biography: *John F. Kennedy*
by Howard S. Kaplan
ISBN 0-7566-0340-4 paperback
ISBN 0-7566-0489-3 hardcover

DK Biography: *Martin Luther King, Jr.*
by Amy Pastan
ISBN 0-7566-0342-0 paperback
ISBN 0-7566-0491-5 hardcover

Look what the critics are saying about DK Biography!

"…highly readable, worthwhile overviews for young people…"—*Booklist*

"This new series from the inimitable DK Publishing brings together the usual brilliant photography with a historian's approach to biography subjects."
—*Ingram Library Services*